ROUGH DIAMONDS

Rough Diamonds

Rethinking How We Educate Future Generations

Dr. Wilfried R. Vanhonacker

HOUNDSTOOTH
PRESS

ROUGH DIAMONDS
Rethinking How We Educate Future Generations

ISBN   978-1-5445-1855-8 *Paperback*
       978-1-5445-1854-1 *Ebook*

To all who gave me opportunities to make mistakes

Contents

Like rough diamonds...
people only become precious...
in the hands of those...
who know how to take care of
them...

—MOHIT K. SINGH

The COVID-19 Pandemic

A Pivotal Moment

This book was formed in my head well before the pandemic emerged and spread around the world. None of my reflections on formal education reported in the book changed in any way because of it. The pandemic has, however, created an opportunity that should not be missed. And that is the opportunity to rethink and redesign pedagogy, so it truly benefits future generations. We owe it to them.

The pandemic has, and continues to have, a devastating effect on many. Schools were forced to close, and there was a massive move from in-classroom teaching to online teaching. Just a few months ago, few of us had ever used or even heard of Zoom. Now, we are all dependent on it to keep our lives tethered.

Education got hit severely and had to figure out how to move forward. Here is where the opportunity lies. As crises accelerate history, cracks that were beginning to form in how we educate are now visible to all. We have to get to work to come out of this better, much better. We can do it if we can get our minds focused on the future. Too many people in education are now trying to figure out how to get back to the good old days. Well, they were good and, in hindsight, better than we realized when we lived them. But they are not coming back. That ship has sailed.

This book was written as a catalyst to inspire thoughts about how we should educate future generations. Because we are at the door of the future, we need to think hard and fast—and move. The past is not coming back, so why bother looking back at it and wondering what might have been? Think and dream about the future. Neither the pandemic nor the pain it has caused should influence our thinking about the future in any way. This book contains some provocative thoughts and reflections about what that future might be like and what it will require from education. We owe it to future generations to think hard and redesign pedagogy for the future, their future. Any effort to hold on to shreds of the past will doom them, us, and that future.

Preface

Why worry about education? Because it has given me so much. My entire career was in higher education, and I was fortunate to have had opportunities in it that many can only dream about. Compared to the typical career path of an academic, mine was a roller coaster ride across the globe: many ups and downs but no shortage of fun and excitement—and more importantly, an incredible journey of reflection and learning.

Riding the tracks of higher education across cultures is part of what made me who I am, and I am grateful for what it has taught me. But I worry about what we do in education, how we do it, and why. Formal education has become a machine on autopilot that tolerates changes at the margin only, and that bothers me greatly. After all, the core responsibility of education is to instill values of learning. How can formal education preserve its credibility if it is incapable and/or unwilling to learn itself?

My background and experiences are in the world of business schools, first as a student and later as a faculty member, dean, and an academic entrepreneur. The latter will sound like an oxymoron to many, but it reflects my many attempts to change education from within. I have the battle scars to prove how difficult that is. In them lies the origin of this book. I believe that education has to become more entrepreneurial and more daring to challenge the status quo. I was very fortunate to have been able to experiment. Not everything worked out as I had planned, but I learned a great deal and my students and colleagues benefited in the process. To me, education should be a dynamic process. Unless we are willing to challenge ourselves and move out of our comfort zones, we have no right being in education. We have to embody and live the role we accepted to play in the life of future generations.

My conviction is firm on the need to reflect and question how we do pedagogy. Our current approach thrives on convenience for the provider and not on a drive to encourage and enhance learning. In fact, the system has outsourced learning and the motivation to learn. But I am getting ahead of myself. We are at a point in time when we need to refocus and take control of the learning process to enhance access, efficiency, and effectiveness for all, including people of all ages, everywhere.

Technological advances provide enormous opportunities to fundamentally reengineer pedagogy (and not, as we do now, increase the footprint and attractiveness of a stale model). We are also at a time when participative engagement thrives because students want—and should—own their learning process. The time for serious reflection (and action) is now; hence, this book. A bit of unorthodox and provocative thinking will do us good, and it can only benefit future generations.

—WILFRIED

Introduction

In the spring of 2017, I spent some time at MIT. My friends at the Sloan School of Management gave me an office where I could camp out for a while. Although the business school was my base, I spent very little time there as I figured I could learn more in and around the university. I divided my time between the university (neuroscience, computer science, and the venerable MIT Media Lab) and the startup ecosystem around it (incubators, accelerators, coworking spaces, etc.). As I wasn't really part of any gig, I could just relax, sit back, observe, and ponder what I saw and experienced. Paradoxically, and a good starting point for reflection, this is a luxury few of us have, but it is also the ideal state for truly learning.

The first thing I noticed was that I was pretty much the only person doing what I was doing. Higher education has become a busy, numbers-driven machine. On a few occasions, I parked myself in a corner of the Sloan School cafeteria and watched the daily spectacle unfold: students, faculty, and staff moving on a clock-driven rhythm like ant colonies between classrooms, labs, work spaces, conference rooms, offices, and the cafeteria. Yes, the cafeteria looked in many ways like a hummingbird feeder; amusing to watch as an outsider, but in no way unique to Sloan. In fact, and something I hadn't realized despite having been part of it for decades, schools and universities have become buzzing beehives, or anything but a calm and relaxing setting that is conducive to learning. I suspect that higher education has become the victim of its own business model and it's trapped in a tunnel with little wiggle room. I can already see the color-coded lines and arrows we see in hospital emergency rooms appear on the floors! Is that where we want to get to? Learning isn't exactly brain surgery in an emergency room!

A second observation I made was looking at and sensing the buildings, the spaces. Perhaps I am overly sensitive, but school buildings are by and large low-energy places. Who wants to spend any time in a classroom outside of class time? Many have no windows, no connection to nature, energy, or real life. Sitting in these empty classrooms feels actually spooky despite wonderful designs and layouts. Many feel like (perhaps telling of the state of affairs of education) morgues; there is just no life in them. Classrooms are designed to brute-force attention on a single point, and that point is definitely not the student! Without us noticing it, education has evolved from classes being conducted outside in the open to students hunkering down in windowless bunkers. At the same time, content has shifted from theoretical posturing and deep thought to practical and everyday relevant materials. The image of an ostrich with its head in the sand comes to mind. We might want to rethink the habitat we conduct education in.

A third observation surprised me but also fascinated me for the promise and potential it holds in rethinking and redesigning learning habitats. Incubators, accelerators, coworking spaces, etc. are really co-learning spaces: more and faster learning goes on in the ecosystem around the university than in the university. From this perspective, classrooms seem more like self-serve delivery stations where little learning occurs; that learning happens (hopefully) elsewhere. We might have lost the co-learning aspect in our educational habitats and turned them into KFC-type delivery outlets; no drive-through (yet) but brain-licking good!

A fourth observation I made was about continuing education, something we must get very serious about soon. The challenge here lies in the realization that our current model of education (what I will refer to as the "all-then-nothing" model) is increasingly at odds with a reality where we live longer, but, at the same time, we become outdated sooner. The observation I made was about executive education, the bread and butter of most business schools. Calibrated across all top business schools, executive education has become largely remedial. It teaches senior executives what they urgently need because they didn't learn about it in the past. It's a penchant for the now created by a deficiency of the past. What about the needs of the future? Education ought to be about preparing and equipping future generations for the future they will encounter. In that sense, education ought to be forward-looking and not backward-correcting.

To stimulate further reflection on this observation, consider that in less than 10 years, at least 50 percent of what MBAs learn will be done by AI-driven intelligent agents. Senior execs will have those agents as part of the teams reporting to them. Teamwork as a subject and learning vehicle is core in any MBA program, but I know of no business school integrating these agents or thinking about what that implies for the human contribution execs will make in an AI-driven collaborative world. Well, more fodder for the perpetual remedial machine, but shouldn't we put the horses before the cart?

A final observation was a fun exercise but, surprisingly, one that few if any business schools have done. It raises questions about how responsive education is to the market, i.e., a reflection on supply and demand. The observation goes well beyond MIT Sloan and holds for most MBA programs. Look 25 years back and compare two things: the core curriculum then with the one of today and the top 20 recruiters then with those of today. Guess what? One hasn't changed much while the other has changed completely. I will let you guess which one is which. But before my inbox flows over, there are plenty of explanations that can be made for this observation. I suspect that most will be defensive in nature, and that is exactly my point. Defensive posturing prevents any learning.

While business schools are the lens through which I view formal education and define my data comfort zone, the concerns I have about formal education go well beyond business schools. My belief is that we desperately need to rethink basic pedagogy to refocus it on enriched and life-long learning for endowed individuals. Without us realizing it, formal education has morphed into a system that is neither intelligent nor being held accountable. That system marches to its own beat irrespective of the reality that unfolds around it. For many of us, inherent talent remains undiscovered or underdeveloped because the system neither attempts to discover it nor adapts to the unique talent and learning profile we all have. Sadly, the focus is on efficient delivery and not on effective learning. In the pursuit of efficient delivery, formal education has become susceptible to dynamics that can easily put the integrity of education (and that of the institutions providing it) at risk. Deep reflection on what we are doing and why is in order, and there is no better time to do it than now.

My objective with this book is to poke at a few aspects of formal education to inspire thought, signal avenues for change, create catalysts for change, and to co-opt you in the process of change. In that process, reflection is healthy and warranted, and this is why I am taking the lead with this book. My reflections on formal education continue to ramify in all sorts of directions that both fascinate and inspire me. Hopefully, they will inspire you to reflect as well. Our collective reflections will likely fuse into imagination and ideas on how to craft a way forward.

I was never the one to accept the status quo. I have been fortunate to be able to experiment, fail, and learn. Curiosity was always the drive, reflection part of the process, and learning the outcome. My reflections come from that experience. They cover aspects of formal education that we rarely question with the aim of triggering further thought and, ultimately, action. And bold action is needed.

This book is not a scientific book in the true sense of what science is and scientists are meant to produce. It is a book of thoughts, questions, and reflections like a series of mental somersaults on the trampoline of my inquisitive mind. As this unscientific wondering naturally implies, my writing will be very different from my academic writing. There will be no data and/or theoretical arguments to disprove well-thought-out hypotheses. I just reflect on observations that I have made during my career in academia and that I continue to make.

The book is also not a piece of art and does not aspire to be one. Writing is laborious and painful for me. My wondering mind is often way ahead of my fingers. The latter just try to catch the tail end of a racing mind and often fail. But that is also why I write; it helps me harness my mind.

Looking at the emerging reality and what it implies for human talent and capabilities that will be needed in the future, I wonder and I worry. I will share many thoughts and lay my worries bare. I will also raise many questions—some unusual, some difficult. Do not expect many answers. The objective is to make you think and reflect. Me giving (or attempting to give) answers would short-circuit your thinking and, therefore, your ability to reflect and learn. As such, the book is not a cookbook. To me, there are no worthwhile challenges that can be addressed with ready-made recipes. If there is a recipe for it, it is no longer a challenge but just a task to be executed.

This book will focus on seven reflections that should stimulate your thinking and inspire action. These reflections are described in random order and are not exhaustive in what occupies my mind on formal education. But they form a basis for some deep thoughts on where we are and what the consequences of that might be. To whet your appetite, here is a quick overview.

1. **Variance**: how much can you learn from somebody who is like you? Variance is a necessary condition for learning to occur. But variance is difficult to work with and because of that, we seem to have traded variance for convenience.

2. **Distance**: looking back in time, creation of knowledge and dissemination of that knowledge have moved away from one another. Indeed, formal education has become a translation/packaging business wedged in between. This has deprived students of experiencing the passion of discovery.

3. **Outsourcing of responsibilities**: responsibilities are being delegated. Parents delegate their responsibilities to educational institutions, and those institutions delegate the learning responsibility to students.

4. **Habitat**: the physical setting of education is not conducive to learning. Most institutions have become huge factories where students tolerate sitting on a production line to get a certification stamp at the end of that line. Classrooms put the teacher at the center, not the student. Many are energy-less bunkers dug into the ground; not exactly inspiring, and as a result, very little learning occurs in them.

5. **Model**: formal education is rigidly bundled within antiquated academic silos. There is little room to wonder across disciplines and learn horizontally.
6. **Content**: what does relevance mean in a rapidly changing world?
7. **Technology**: we are using technology to shore up outdated pedagogy instead of embracing its capabilities to fundamentally reengineer pedagogy.

We really ought to think more and deeper about what we are doing in formal education and why.

As reflections are triggered by context and shaped by experiences and beliefs, I will first describe the context we find ourselves in. My focus there will be on two aspects: first, the necessary pursuit of higher-order learning and the challenges we face today to achieve that; and second, the emerging reality that necessitates true lifelong learning and requires a paradigm shift in education. That discussion will be followed by an account of my own journey and the experiences that shaped my reflections and define my data comfort zone. Before laying out those reflections, I will share some basic beliefs that I hold about human talent and the responsibilities of formal education to discover, develop, and weaponize that talent. Following my reflections, I will delve deeper into lifelong learning as the starting point in reconfiguring formal education, formal education's business model, and the need for accountability in education. The book concludes with a discussion on where we should go from here.

You do not need to read the reflections in the order they appear in the book. Just jump in where your curiosity leads you. But read my path and beliefs before you do jump in. Reflections are not reproductions of observations or experiences but are reconstructions of them. That process of reconstruction is dependent on context. Without knowing that context, reflections cannot be fully understood and appreciated. I was very fortunate to have had a rich career in education, and because of this, I have reflections that are both broad and deep.

Read the book and think about the observations I make and the questions I raise. Reflect on my reflections. Let your mind wonder, but keep it open and try to turn off all defensive reflexes. Or, at the very least, recognize them when they start blocking your thinking. It is about stretching the mind to bring transparency to something that is fundamental to being intelligent. Write down your own thoughts and reflections. Learning requires a bit of mental surgery on experiences, and writing sharpens the scalpel. Writing does sharpen the mind. Be sure to share your thoughts and reflections online with the community of concerned souls. Together, we can and will move mountains. We owe it to future generations.

CHAPTER ONE

Where We Find Ourselves

Education finds itself in a very challenging environment. Infinite access to information not only necessitates but also requires a heavy dose of critical thinking, the aim in higher-order learning. At the same time, a new reality is emerging that will shake education to its core.

EDUCATION AND HIGHER-ORDER LEARNING

Formal education, or what we colloquially refer to as "going to school," is a major piece in the puzzle to shape and achieve higher-order learning. But formal education does not occur in a vacuum. Everyday experiences play a role as well. Reflecting on these experiences and mentally dissecting them constitutes learning. Formal education helps sharpen the scalpel to achieve more profound learning from our everyday experiences.

Higher-order learning, also known as higher-order thinking, aims to stimulate deeper thinking and more cognitive processing. Center to that is critical thinking: the ability to think independently and do it in a critical manner. My focus here will be on formal education in its quest to develop critical thinking. To set the stage and bring color to the discussion, it is quite educational to reflect on critical thinking when all of us have access to infinite amounts of data, info, opinions, etc. anytime of the day. On one hand, this reality puts the urgency for critical thinking in sharper focus. On the other hand, what info exactly reaches us poses a real threat to encouraging and developing critical thinking. Before digging in, let me first illustrate the urgent need for critical thinking from my recent experience teaching university undergraduates.

In my teaching, I require all students to bring their tech toys to class, often in violation of school policy at the places I teach. Particularly with younger crowds, I feel I need to step into their world to connect with them. Technology can be disruptive and undermine attention, but only if you let it do so. To just right out ban it deprives learning in the reality these students will have to be operational in. I never saw myself as competing with their screens. I use them in a collaborative learning process that students seem to appreciate. More importantly, they learn some valuable lessons in the process. So, I moved away from anchoring my teaching on my screen to anchoring it on their screens. Of course, multiple screens imply variance, as the probability that they all see the same thing is virtually zero. But, as I will point out throughout this book, variance is where learning hides. Without variance, there cannot be any learning. An illustration will make this clear.

When I ask my business school undergraduates what they think the market capitalization (or cap, for short) of Apple is, some venture a number. It is a number I do not expect them to know, but one that they should be able to make an intelligent guess about. A good unit to consider would be billions of dollars, and they should know that Apple is a big, well-performing company (many are sitting there with the latest iPhone, so the company ought to benefit from this somewhere!). I also expect them to be aware of the fact that the trillion-dollar mark was surpassed recently (first by Amazon).

The numbers they come up with in response to my question are usually low. To push them a little, I name two or three other companies they would know in different industries and ask them whether they think the market cap of these companies is larger or smaller than Apple's. This should give them a better feel for the numbers they come up with. In my experience, few have a real feel for what $100 billion or $200 billion is in market cap. They don't really know whether that is big or small. These are numbers they can read but not really relate to and/or evaluate in any particular context.

My probing gets us into a discussion of what a market cap is and how it is derived. As they begin to look at me, expecting me to tell them what the number is, I tell them, "I don't know" (by that time, they are familiar with me and my teaching style!). I tell them to look up Apple's market cap on their devices. After all, the answer to all questions these days is "Google knows!" They invariably come up with multiple numbers. I then tell them that only one number can be correct, that I do not know that number (I only really have a vague idea of what it is), and that it is possible that none of the numbers they came up with is the correct one. Then, I tell them to figure out what the correct number is. At that point, most don't know where to start. This requires info literacy and some critical thinking, core requirements for our times.

Note also that my role as a teacher is changing in this collaborative approach. The change in role of teachers (educators) and educational institutions is something I will push further later in the book as I reflect on formal education. I believe their roles will change, but I need to put a few more foundations in place before we can build on that argument and explore what that new role might be.

The threat to encouraging and developing critical thinking lies in what exactly pops up on our screens. In many ways, the algorithms online platforms use to filter and control what we see feed off our worst instincts. Let me explore this a bit so we understand what formal education is up against when it comes to thinking and achieving higher-order learning in the information age.

The problem lies in that feed algorithms learn who we are and then filter out anything that does not quite fit who they think we are and might want to see. In their quest to personalize, they narrow access and more so as they get to know us better. The net result is the creation of digital echo chambers that reinforce what we already know, believe, and do. The personal tailoring has benefits, but it runs counter to developing (or encouraging) critical thinking. In fact, to stimulate deeper thought, the educational thing to do would be to feed us different and/or opposing views from the ones we already hold; in other words, the exact opposite of what these feed algorithms currently do.

Unfortunately (and a bit alarmingly), the way these algorithms are designed leads them to feed us views already aligned with ours, but with the extreme crowding out the more moderate. As they get to know us better, the variance in what we see goes down and the mean shifts out to a more polarized position. There is indeed the real danger that feed algorithms drive extremism in any shape or form.

Make no mistake about it, many of these feed algorithms are driven by engines that know us very well (often better than we know ourselves). As we all become more dependent on online access to stay "informed," we might want to reflect on this dynamic. As educators, we should reflect on this and its implications as well. In our pursuit to achieve higher-order thinking, we have our work cut out for us.

There is of course a question of whether all students have the capability to develop critical thinking. It requires a certain mindset and intellectual ability. Just look at the "adults" (and I add the quotes for a reason) around you. Many don't have it or seem incapable and/or unwilling to exercise it; this is often after years of formal education and life experiences. Claws of prejudice, ideology, etc. have grasped their brains and made them unable to develop into the truly wonderful organs they are. Formal education ought to stretch the brain, untangle the knots, and pull out claws that might prevent it from developing into the wonderful and powerful organ we uniquely possess as human beings. Brains are muscles that need to be stretched to remain fully functional. Stretching is what critical thinking is all about. Without it, all learning ceases. As I will discuss next, we are rapidly entering into a reality where continued learning (and continued challenges) will become the core of our life's journey. Without it, we will be left behind.

THE EMERGING REALITY

The model of formal education that we have all become accustomed to is one where we get our formal education early in life and then put that to some productive use until retirement. For those of us who aspire to graduate from college, formal education stops when we are about 21 to 25 years old. If the retirement age is 60, we expect a productive career of 35 years, or roughly twice the length of our formal education. I will refer to this as the "all-then-nothing" model. Of course, I put it a bit extremely as some will go back to school for retraining or continued education later in life, either by desire or necessity. But the basic "all-then-nothing" model describes life's journey for most of us. We have come to accept that model without much thought on whether or not it is sustainable, especially in the emerging reality we face.

The reality is that we are experiencing change at an accelerating pace. I believe that the changes we see and experience today are just the beginning of an age of perpetual disruption. Just look across industries and see how innovations in technologies and business models have turned once-vibrant sectors into dinosaurs almost overnight. And education will not be spared. Whatever shape or form these changes occur in, we already notice that the knowledge we acquired in school gets outdated quickly. Across disciplines, we become historians and/or curators of dated knowledge without realizing it.

This is basically nothing new. When I was in college studying applied economics and econometrics, I had an older macroeconomics professor who was teaching us as if the gold standard was still scaffolding global economies! Outdated faculty are not a new phenomenon, and all of us who spent any time in academia will recognize (hopefully only a few) colleagues of that mold. But the problem is going on steroids! The fact is that many fields progress so fast today that unless we stay on top, we will become outdated in no time. Plus, this will get worse as the process of innovation and development accelerates.

At the same time, life expectancies are generally on the rise. Thanks to medical and other advances, we can all look forward to living to a ripe old age. With aging populations in most industrialized nations, we now see retirement ages creeping up as well. This means we are moving into a reality of getting outdated faster while having to work longer. Given that reality, we need to fundamentally rethink how formal education should be woven into the fabric of our lives. The all-then-nothing model does not fit with that reality and can only be a recipe for disaster.

We need to stop thinking of lifelong learning as a necessary add-on to, or an extension of, a deficient model. We need a new model altogether. That model is likely to change the roles of students, educators, and educational institutions. Since education is a lead sector, we really have no time to relax, and we'd better start reinventing ourselves with a mission for the future (or get out of the way). In all honesty, I am not sure exactly what model will emerge and/or prevail, but I can think of one characteristic it most likely will have: a focus on learning how to learn and the development of a persistent passion for learning.

WHY THIS BOOK AND WHY NOW?

Education is important. It is crucial to the development of human intelligence. Nature gives us capabilities, but it is up to us to convert those capabilities into competencies that can be leveraged in rewarding ways. Raw intelligence is something that needs to be worked on. Although formal education plays an important role in that process, the underlying question motivating this book is: "How good of a job is formal education doing at that?" It is worth stepping back and considering that question now as we enter an era where continuous and enhanced learning will become pivotal.

Human beings are like raw diamonds: they have potential, but the inherent beauty and value emerge only with a perfect cut; i.e., a cut that recognizes that unique potential and that will bring out the sparkle nature deposited in the stone. How well is formal education as we know it today doing in cutting human diamonds? Do we sparkle to our full potential? We should take a step back and reflect on these questions. The time to do this is now as a new and emerging reality raises serious questions about the ability of formal education to instill and encourage a culture of learning. Formal education has become a big machine that marches to its own beat in a reality that is changing rapidly and drastically. Many of the things we do in formal education are based on assumptions that were perhaps valid at some time in the past, but are they still valid? Are we still on course, or have we veered off course?

The urgency to think and reflect is particularly acute because education is a lead sector and education should develop talent today that will be needed tomorrow. It is not enough to develop it when it is needed; it should be ready to be deployed when it is needed. Any deficiencies today will manifest themselves tomorrow. Just think of the consequences when a lead sector is disrupted! We might only see perpetual remedial efforts, some of which we already see today. We educate future generations for the future *they* will face. We should look into that future (no matter how difficult that is) and work backward to see and evaluate if the machine is doing what it is supposed to be doing. Ironically, a dose of critical thinking is needed in our pursuit of critical thinking.

By nature, I tend to be a critical person. It also comes with my training as a scientist, but criticism seldom inspires. It tends to trigger defensive posturing and shut minds. I want this book to spark thought, deep thought. I want to go back together with you and think about formal education and its role in learning, especially lifelong learning. Questioning will stretch our minds, and in the process, it will bring transparency to issues that require serious reflection. This book is meant to be a catalyst for thought and an inspiration for change.

CHAPTER TWO

My Journey and Data Comfort Zone

My academic career path was anything but normal. It brought me opportunities most can only dream about, and I took pretty much all of them. After all, opportunities seldom come back when you take a pass on them. Taking opportunities also leads to more opportunities. My path wasn't smooth; it brought many challenges, setbacks, and disappointments. An emotional roller coaster. Because the highs and lows undoubtedly color my views and reflections, I have the obligation to pull the curtain back and let you peek into my past. Variance in experiences implies a richness learning can only benefit from. Variance is a theme I will repeatedly come back to, since learning requires variance. I wouldn't necessarily say that I maximized it in my career, but I certainly went a few standard deviations beyond what a typical academic would experience in her or his career. Let me roll back the tape of my journey.

My first contact with formal education came when I was seven years old and started grade one. The school building was a temporary wooden shack with one classroom that, if I remember correctly, housed grades one and two together. My only memory of that time was the teacher. She was a nun dressed in the traditional Catholic nun regalia who had just returned from Africa. I do not recall, but no doubt this nun told us fascinating stories about her experiences as a missionary in Africa. The passion that usually comes with recounting personal experiences might well have planted the seed for my own future adventures. Nothing is more memorable or motivating in the learning process than the passion a teacher brings to his or her class.

My subsequent education was pretty much following in the footsteps of my brother, the oldest of seven siblings. We both went through the same Catholic high school (boys only, of course) and on to study applied economics with the Jesuits at UFSIA in Antwerp (Belgium). College was a time of discovery for me and one that set me on a path that diverged from my brother's and laid the groundwork for a career in academia. Before I go into that, let me reflect on my upbringing from a youngster until my college years.

I grew up in a large family shaped by the remnants of two world wars. My parents grew up in Flanders, Belgium. Both were young teenagers when WWII broke out, very much like their parents were when WWI ravished their ancestral homes. Their formal education ended with high school. Despite their limited formal education, my parents understood the importance of a good education and gave all of us the opportunities they could afford, and then some they barely could afford. Finances were constantly a struggle, but my siblings and I didn't know it at the time. We were happy kids shielded from a harsh reality. Despite their hardships, or perhaps because of them, my parents gave me and my siblings a solid upbringing.

Looking back, our childhoods evolved around three activities that shaped all of us. One was the Catholic schooling we received all the way through high school. That schooling shaped my moral compass, one that has been tested severely in my academic career. I never wavered from the values instilled in me by my early education and the ones my parents lived by every day of their lives. Another activity that shaped me early on was the Boy Scouts. Both my brother and I joined them (my sisters all joined the Girl Scouts). The many years and adventures with the Boy Scouts taught me discipline, duty, and teamwork. To this day, I still make my bed every day (even in the hotels I stay in!). The third activity we all engaged in was attending the local art academy, which I did on evenings and weekends all the way through high school. Working with artists shaped my vision, aesthetic appreciation, and gave me a keen and perceptive eye for detail. All these were rock solid foundations I took with me to college in 1972, and I still benefit from them to this day.

A few months after my mom passed away, I started college. My dad drove me to my dorm. It was the only time he came to Antwerp during the four years I was there. But I distinctly remember when he parked the car in front of the dorm and turned off the engine. I cannot recall at all what we talked about driving over, but what he said before I got out of the car stuck with me.

Peering over the steering wheel, he said, "I can give you only one chance."

Dad was never a person who wasted words, so when he said something, we paid attention. I doubt I fully understood what he was saying at the time, but it registered. His words have stayed with me ever since. I certainly understand today what he was saying and why. I do not recall feeling any pressure, but college is certainly where I found my passion. That only chance was about to take me on an extraordinary career.

At the end of my second year in college, I opted for the more challenging math track—econometrics—and discovered that I enjoyed it and was pretty good at it. It wouldn't be the last time that I went for the more difficult option. Although I was a good student all through middle school and high school, I never really made it to the top of any class. But I graduated college at the top of my class. I reveled in the challenge to beat the odds and get it done. Academics appealed to me. I liked working on difficult problems with a stubborn persistence. More importantly, I found inspiration in working with a young faculty member who had just returned from MIT. Nothing is more motivating than an inspiring role model.

Straight out of college and never having taken a course in English, I started my PhD in marketing science at the Krannert School of Management, Purdue University in the fall of 1976. At that time, it was one of the best places to be in that field and I was lucky to get in. As was customary, to earn my tuition I had to teach undergraduate students in the business school. Yes, you get the picture—a freshly-graduated undergraduate teaching undergraduates in a foreign language in a foreign country! In hindsight, it was fun. It was my first experience being an educator, and I had no clue what that meant at that time (by the end of this book, you will be able to judge whether I have made progress on that front). What saved me was being clever (I used a textbook different from the one the students had) and having a good sense of humor. I have never taken myself too seriously and have always surrounded myself with people who feel and act the same way. For me, pride is an asset; ego is not. Perspective and a good sense of humor are valued, and I have lived (and continue to live) by these principles. A few years later, when I was teaching at Columbia University, an MBA student wrote on my teaching evaluation that if I wasn't going to make it in academia, I certainly would as a stand-up comedian!

My PhD studies were hard, but they taught me the right academic values and ones that I would benefit from throughout my career. I defended my dissertation in the summer of 1979, signed off, deposited my thesis in the library, jumped in a U-Haul truck, and drove to New York City for my first job ever as a newly minted professor. The Graduate School of Business at Columbia University had offered me a position as assistant professor in their marketing department. Looking back, it was the only time in my career when I had to actually look for a job. Pretty much all the opportunities I have had since then just came to me. I have been lucky and blessed in that way.

At Columbia University, I did pretty much what all fresh PhD candidates embarking on an academic research career do—I did research and taught. The latter was not a priority. I distinctly remember the dean of the school telling the new faculty recruits that the objective for teaching was to keep the students out of his office! But teaching duties bring some structure and grounding to the all-consuming and solitary world of basic academic research. While spending some time in New York City in 2018, I went back to visit some of my former colleagues, now all distinguished scholars. Some of them were still in the same office doing the same thing (and still doing it very well). It made me think and reflect on how my career path had veered away from theirs. I have enormous respect and admiration for what they do and have achieved, but I feel they missed out on a lot of what life can offer along with the learning and growth that comes with that. My adventure started in Uris Hall in the mid-1980s.

One day, a senior colleague walked into my office and asked me whether I was interested in going to China. Talk about a question coming out of left field! In between math modeling and tedious computer simulations, there was no time to think about any travel, let alone to China. Little did I know at that time that my world was about to change. On Christmas Eve 1985, I arrived in Beijing. A couple of days later, I flew to Lhasa (Tibet) for the start of a trip through the western part of China.

What had made all this possible was the following: one of the industrial ministries (still operating at the time) had selected a group of about 40 promising students for an MBA-type program. They had reached out to senior faculty at Columbia University to staff the program. But each module was two months long, and my senior colleague could only go for a couple of weeks. That's when he asked me to fill in for the remaining time. My teaching schedule enabled me to do this and off I went. I had assumed that this would be a one-off, so I had taken the map of China and decided to visit the western part prior to my teaching, and the eastern part when my teaching was done. Little did I know how difficult it was to travel in China at that time. But I made it and I am glad I did it. During my two months in China, I got to know the country, the people, and the culture. I fell for it. Upon returning to Columbia University, I started learning Chinese to develop a deeper understanding of the culture. My ambition at the time was to be able to teach in Chinese, something I have regrettably not achieved yet.

As I got invited back, I started spending a couple of months every year in China as a foreign expert ("foreign" definitely, "expert" not sure!). While in Beijing, I got involved with the China-Europe Management Institute (CEMI). CEMI was a 10-year development-aid project financed by the European Union (EU). Starting in 1984, it was one of the very early MBA-type programs in China. As a member of its Academic Council and later as its acting dean, we started thinking about turning that program into a fully-fledged independent business school. It was a daring dream to say the least. Education has always been one of the more ideologically conservative bastions in the Chinese government. Foreign involvement in that sector turned all the lights on red in Beijing. That dream led to the creation of CEIBS, China's leading business school and the first non-European, non-North American business school today with its MBA ranked in the top 25 in the world by the *Financial Times*. The incredible success it is today, CEIBS grew out of CEMI and the daring dream a few of us had in the late '80s.

The creation of CEIBS is a fascinating story, but not one to focus on here. It was bold and many pieces had to fall in place to make it a reality; fortunately, they did. Just think of the odds of pulling this off in the '90s when your students were in Tiananmen Square on June 4, 1989! I learned a lot in the process, and I am proud of the role I played in it. I was offered the founding deanship but declined. I thought it was too early in my academic career to move into a full-time administrative role. I stayed on the Academic Council and eventually did become their dean in the late '90s to help build the nucleus of the permanent faculty CEIBS needed to sustain its rapid growth.

With my passion for China growing, I left Columbia University for INSEAD in the fall of 1988. I wanted to be at a business school with a more global outlook and one that saw and understood that China was going to become an important player in the world. It also helped that my college idol had left UFSIA to assume the deanship at INSEAD with an ambition to bring more of an academic research culture to the independent business school.

INSEAD was going through a transition when I was on its faculty. One topic of great debate at the time is relevant to this book and the reflections I will make on formal education. INSEAD was exploring the creation of a hub in Asia, a move I supported strongly. I pushed forward two points in the debate, neither of which saw the light of day. The first point was to make a bold move and put the hub in China; eventually, the hub was created in Singapore. Perhaps I had a biased perspective with one of my feet in China already. My argument was that Singapore is in Asia but is not Asia. In the end, risk-averse attitudes and convenience arguments tipped the scale in favor of Singapore. No doubt a China hub would have been very different from the successful base INSEAD has in Singapore today.

The other point I argued for in the discussion on an Asian hub was not to use the export model but to use the import model. To me, re-creating INSEAD in Asia would be a missed opportunity. My point was that we should experiment with novel ideas (within the boundaries of what the INSEAD brand stood for) and bring those that worked back to the main campus in Fontainebleau. I saw the Asian hub not just as an ambitious extension but as an opportunity for the institute to reinvent itself. In short, it was an opportunity to learn.

As the '90s rolled in, I was getting anxious to get closer to Asia, especially China. An opportunity arose with the creation of the University of Science and Technology (known today as HKUST) in Hong Kong. The Anderson School at UCLA played an advisory role in the establishment of the business school at HKUST, and colleagues there asked me to go and build the marketing department in the business school. This was an excellent opportunity at the time, as I could be on China's doorstep but maintain solid footing in the academic world. I would eventually leave HKUST to take up the deanship at CEIBS, but in the early '90s, I was not ready yet to plunge into a full-time administrative role. At the time, I still had a few papers to write! HKUST provided academic credibility and a platform to deploy my entrepreneurial talent. A curiosity and drive to build had been emerging, but I felt that I needed a stronger academic record before lifting the anchor. As Steve Jobs famously put it, "Why join the navy if you can be a pirate?" My pirate genes were getting restless.

When the deanship at CEIBS opened up, I took an academic leave from HKUST and moved to Shanghai. I wasn't exactly sure if I was dean material (and had little understanding of what that actually meant or entailed), but I was very familiar with CEIBS and felt I could hit the ground running. With what we had achieved at HKUST, I was also confident that we could recruit professors and start building the nucleus of a resident faculty, which CEIBS sorely needed. That was not an easy task, but persistence and sticking to core academic values helped. Of course, we benefited greatly from the rise of China. It was no longer the China I discovered when I first arrived in Beijing on Christmas Eve 1985. China had awakened and as Napoleon famously predicted, it would shake the world when it did.

When I took on the dean's position at CEIBS, I learned something very quickly—I was no longer feeling the pulse of the organization. I knew the place well, but the day I moved into the dean's office, many lines of communication went dead or became filtered. The change was quite dramatic. Having been part of the project from its inception, I knew what was going on and heard it all until I officially became dean. Now I understood what it really meant when someone said, "It's lonely at the top."

After a few years as dean at CEIBS, I went back to my academic perch at HKUST. I had some thinking to do. What next? My learning curve in China was flattening and headhunters were all over me for deanships, a job that in the best of circumstances is not easy. I did not want to be a dean to be somebody. If I was going to be a dean again, I wanted to do something meaningful. I wanted to create, build, and move boundaries with a drive and eagerness that has motivated me ever since. I was also beginning to question what we did in business schools. Some of the reflections I will share with you started fermenting at that time.

Headhunters knew that I wasn't a typical dean's candidate. I wasn't the guy to move a big-name school one or two degrees left or right. So, a London-based firm inquired about a job to build a new business school in Russia. Russia? That was pretty much my reaction at the time. A reaction not unlike the one I had when my senior colleague at Columbia University had asked me about going to China years earlier. As was the case with China at that time, there was absolutely nothing about Russia on my radar screen. Following the collapse of the USSR, I had done some executive education in Moscow for an INSEAD client, but that was the extent of my experience with Russia. The opportunity was truly unique and intriguing, one that an academic could only dream about.

One of Russia's most-respected businessmen, together with a few of his friends, wanted to build the business school of the future. With Kremlin support (the prime minister at the time was the chairman of the school's board) and the commitment of significant resources, the goal was to create something new. They had visited the top business schools around the world and didn't like what they saw. As is often the case in such situations, they knew what they didn't want but didn't quite know exactly what they wanted. Ambition, resources, and a clean sheet of paper; it was a no-brainer for me even though I was jumping off a cliff without much of a parachute. A few months later, I was off to Moscow for a new adventure. My friends in Hong Kong and China were now convinced that I had finally lost it. In their eyes, I had lifted the anchor and thrown it overboard!

The five years I spent in Moscow building the foundations of the Moscow School of Management (MSM) SKOLKOVO, or what would become Russia's leading private business school, were an incredible experience. When I arrived, I didn't know a word of Russian and very little if anything about the local culture and practices. I just dove in and tried to learn to swim as fast as I could. We had a tough task ahead of us: building a new business school from scratch in a place that is not exactly known for business schools. What we did have was resources, energy, and an ambition to build a new benchmark. We had no role model to go by and had to build the credibility fast that Russia could do this and that it was the place to do it. We set out to build an entirely new MBA program, one that would articulate our vision for MSM SKOLKOVO. That vision was to develop entrepreneurial leaders for difficult environments. Accordingly, we were going to turn the harsh reality of Russia into the cornerstone of the new school's identity.

Our focus was very much on a full-time MBA program, the flagship program of most business schools. We started with a clean slate, but I felt that we had to keep a few reference points that people were familiar with, otherwise nobody would take us seriously. I very quickly brought in MIT's Sloan School as a strategic partner to gain visibility and credibility to what we were doing. The Sloan School was keen on coming along to learn with us. We were going to move boundaries in ways an established school could not unless they were willing to put their reputation on the line. We, in contrast, had nothing to lose but everything to gain.

One element of the attraction for me to go to Russia was that the founder was adamant about not getting involved with accreditation. Over the years, I have been quite vocal in my criticism of accreditations and how they stifle innovation and creativity, something that I felt was sorely needed. Why re-create Harvard or Sloan? Where would one get the audacity to assume that one could beat these schools at their own game? Playing their game (and increasingly the game of accreditation agencies themselves) would at best make a good copycat school. If we wanted to rise to the top, we had to change the game in a meaningful and credible way. There are so many things we naturally understand as kids but forget as adults—the easiest way to win a game is to set the rules. We were ready to set new rules as we defined our ambitions for MSM SKOLKOVO.

One challenge for any new school or university is to create gravity: attract good and qualified students, staff, and faculty. The faculty is a core element in building academic credibility for a new institution. I was well aware that Moscow wasn't very high on the list of places in the world where one could build an academic career. One idea I worked on for a while was to merge the leading private business school in each of the BRIC countries: FDC in Brazil, ISB in India, Changjiang in China, and SKOLKOVO in Russia. The BRICs were still hot and all represented difficult environments (but each in their own, unique way), thus, they fit our mission. All four institutions had the same challenges when it came to recruiting faculty with global academic credibility. Creating a new global business school with one foot in each of the BRIC countries might be an attractive proposition. It would certainly get a lot of attention and potentially be a game changer. The ability to move students, staff, and faculty around the globe had a nice ring to it! We were already collaborating with each institution, so why not explore a closer integration or even a full merger? There was no shortage of excitement! We didn't get very far because of politics and egos, however, and there were too many loose ends in Moscow that might come unraveled at any moment. But I still think about what a great school that might have been.

After spending five years in Moscow, I needed a break. Building MSM SKOLKOVO was physically and emotionally exhausting; my tires were flat. I also wanted to take some time off to reflect on my experience, rewind the tape and go over the many decisions I had made over the years. I moved to the French countryside to read and write (and have a glass of wine). I pretty much wrote a whole book on my Moscow stint. Writing is very therapeutic, but it is also a necessary step in learning from experience. Putting things on paper requires sharp thought and deep reflection.

I also faced the question of: "What next?" How does one top the opportunity and experience I had had in Moscow and Shanghai? As you will understand by now, I wasn't going to take the easy route! There was still plenty to discover and learn. As the headhunters were on my path again, I narrowed my interests to two parts of the world I knew little about but that intrigued me. One was the Central Asian republics, especially Kazakhstan an emerging economy wedged in between two giants, Russia and China. Knowing a bit about both, I was curious how they leveraged their geographic position given a richness in natural resources both neighbors needed. The other part of the world that intrigued me was the Arab world. Despite it being a region with a high concentration of young people, it had no universities or business schools with a truly global reputation. I wondered why that was the case.

An opportunity to find out presented itself when I was asked about taking on the deanship of the Olayan School of Business at the American University of Beirut (AUB) in Beirut (Lebanon). The school had gone through some turmoil and seasoned leadership was needed to get it back on track and realize some of the potential it had. This was a turnaround job within a university setting, something new and something I could learn from. After a year of reflection and writing in the French countryside, I moved to Beirut. The day I arrived in Beirut, the chief of security in the country was assassinated. Not a reassuring sign and, I thought, hopefully not an omen for what was to come. But I was all in, which, to me, is the only way to lead an institution credibly.

Lebanon is a beautiful country and one of the few places in the world where you can go to the beach in the morning and go skiing in the afternoon. Unfortunately, lack of political leadership and mismanagement have pushed it to the brink of economic collapse. A failed state wrapped in the cloth of foreign donations without which it could not survive. Years of civil war left deep scars and continue to cast long shadows over the society. For most Lebanese, daily life is a struggle most non-Lebanese would never put up with under any circumstance. The harsh reality dampens one's perspective. If everyday life is a struggle, you don't look at the horizon (and certainly not beyond). You lose perspective as the reality unfolding around you grows on you. This was a rude awakening for me. It was further complicated by the fact that anything you said or touched was immediately caught in the vicious claws of sectarian politics. This was not for me. I left the dean's office and went on a sabbatical to MIT. It was time to recharge the batteries after they had slowly run down trying to be a force of change in a world that seems to move only in circles.

My reflections on formal education started percolating in my mind while I roamed around Cambridge. That's when I made two decisions: first, I would take early retirement from academia as too many things beyond it were torturing the roots of my understanding, i.e., I had to lift anchor to stay intellectually alive. Second, the startup scene was too inviting not to jump into. Never too old to kick crazy ideas in the gut and see how far they would roll, I started working on an intelligent decision-support platform. The motivation to get into this came from my interest in novel business models for higher education. I believe that the current model is not sustainable. More importantly, adherence to the current model warps mindsets that should know better. The prevailing business model has become the sail by which many institutions hold a steady course. But more on that later. The decision-support platform has a curating mechanism that grows talent in its ecosystem. Hence, I wandered off the path of academia but not off the path of talent development.

CHAPTER THREE

Basic Beliefs About Education

My views on formal education are underpinned by two basic beliefs. The first belief I hold is that we are all born with a natural gift waiting to be discovered and developed. In other words, I believe that we are all born as rough diamonds. The second belief I hold is that all those with a learning mindset should have access to affordable education that enables them to develop their natural gift to its full potential.

BASIC BELIEFS

We are all born as rough diamonds, waiting to be discovered, waiting to be studied, waiting to be cut to reveal the natural sparkle we inherently have. That also holds true for those with physical and/or mental challenges. There is evidence that suggests they often show remarkable talent as if there is a natural process of compensation at work—a loss in one area leads to a gain in another. Consider deaf Beethoven, epileptic Dostoyevsky, blind Huxley, dyslexic Galileo, and ADHD Einstein, and the list goes on. As is the case with natural diamonds, very few of us have no flaws or imperfections. Still, despite these deficiencies, most diamonds can be cut into remarkable stones. If we care to look, potential is hidden in each of us and that potential is a whole world waiting to be discovered.

As with rough diamonds, no two stones are exactly alike and offer exactly the same potential. The inherent sparkle we are born with is specific and unique to each and every one of us. For some of us, our natural gift falls in the intellectual domain. For others, their natural gift could be a refined artistic talent, an innate athletic ability, or some other extraordinary ability. We are not all born Einsteins, but we are all born with a unique gift that holds potential, and that potential needs to be truly discovered for it to be understood and appreciated.

The analogy to diamonds is quite instructive and revealing. I will keep coming back to it as I reflect on formal education and its role in bringing rough diamonds to sparkle. Just allow me to make two observations from the diamond industry that are relevant and that should put us on a path of reflection. First, near-perfect stones are studied for a very long time before they are touched in any way. This is done to make sure that the eventual cut decided upon reveals the stone's potential in the best way. Second, although flaws and imperfections are nearly always there, the focus is never on those deficiencies but on the potential that nature has endowed each stone with. In the end, they all sparkle with beauty, forever.

Just as not all rough diamonds are cut exactly the same way, I also believe that not all of us qualify for the same type of formal education. Specifically, I do not see formal education as an unconditional human right. What I do believe is that any type of formal education should be accessible to those who have the gift that that particular type of education can develop. As with rough diamonds, it is the inherent potential we are endowed with that should determine what formal education we should have access to.

In contrast to rough diamonds, however, human beings are not mindless stones. They possess mindsets that can help, but also block, any attempt at shaping them. To truly benefit from formal education, that education should be fully aligned with their natural talent, and they should possess a mindset that enables that education to bring out the full potential of their natural talent. Accordingly, what I believe is that anybody with a gift for music and a mindset to develop it should have access to music education.

Anybody exceptionally handy at craftwork and a desire to devote himself/herself to developing that skill to perfection should have access to expertise to do so. Anybody with an intellectual ability and a passion and commitment to develop that ability should have access to higher education. Accordingly, endowment is necessary but not sufficient. To benefit from any education and for education to succeed in bringing out a person's full potential, that person should have a mindset amenable to learning. I will refer to such a mindset as the learning mindset.

In a nutshell, my beliefs are that we all have a unique gift and that we all should have access to affordable education to develop that gift to its full potential, conditional on having acquired a learning mindset. Therefore, a learning mindset is a necessary requirement to be able to exercise one's right of access to formal education. As I will discuss later, talent and mindset are necessary to protect the integrity of education. Let us first explore what I mean by a learning mindset and where such a mindset comes from.

THE LEARNING MINDSET

For any type of formal education to be able to effectively develop inherent talent, students should possess a learning mindset. As we all surely remember from our schooling days, education is not a picnic. It requires concentration, persistence, and effort. I vividly remember days (well, mostly nights) when I was pursuing my PhD, and I threw my books against the wall of my student cubicle in frustration. I could make neither head nor tail on a math problem that I had to conquer. I would scream and yell, drop a tear, go for a walk, come back, sit down behind my desk, hunker down, and dig in again. There is just no easy way around it. Formal education of any type and at all ages is hard work. As Nicolas Sparks reminds us, "Nothing that is worthwhile is ever easy."

What is a learning mindset, exactly? Here are some of my thoughts on what makes a learning mindset:

- A curious and inquisitive mind: thirst for knowledge is a good motivator for putting in the necessary effort and sticking with it. In fact, for a curious and inquisitive mind, the required effort is neither seen nor felt; it becomes a labor of love.
- A passion for learning: any form of education is a journey, often long and lonely. One really has to enjoy the process as much as the outcome.
- An awareness and understanding that learning requires focus, patience, persistence, and commitment.
- Self-motivation and self-drive: one needs to be on a mission and derive pleasure and motivation from moving toward an objective.

This learning mindset needs to be present as you set off on

a learning journey. It has to be something a student has already acquired when he/she gets into the starting blocks. That implies that it should be shaped prior to starting any type of formal education. Accordingly, it is not education's responsibility to instill such a mindset. Education's responsibility is to harness it, leverage it, and, if possible, turbocharge it. How is a learning mindset then acquired, and whose responsibility is it to instill such a mindset?

Parents set the scene that will shape their children's mindsets. Parents should behave like conductors of an orchestra where values, beliefs, and experiences are tuned and aligned to create a learning mindset. Note that I wrote "should"; acquiring a learning mindset is a parental responsibility and one that cannot easily be outsourced. I will comment on the latter later in the book as there seems to be quite a bit of outsourcing going on in and around formal education, and that should worry all of us. But for now, let me stick with the parents' responsibility to develop a learning mindset in children. To give some perspective on the challenge in instilling such a learning mindset in children, let me take a step back and reflect on parenting and parental responsibilities in general.

Anybody who has gone through a formal child adoption process knows how demanding that process is. Adoptive parents are put through all kinds of tests and interviews to assess whether they fully understand their responsibilities toward the adopted child. Part of that assessment focuses on views around and about education. The whole process is long and often frustrating. Of course, adoption agencies (and governments in the case of international adoptions) want to assure themselves that the adoptive parents have the child's welfare at heart. No doubt, there have been abuses that justify the adoptive parents being X-rayed from top to bottom and from front to back. Having gone through an international adoption as an adoptive parent myself, every step of the process is wholly justified even when disbelief and frustration take the upper hand at times. The whole experience makes you think carefully about what you are embarking on and what your responsibilities are and will be as the child grows up. There is just no way to go through the whole adoption process and not develop an acute understanding of what it is to be a parent.

Now, let me bring the curveball back into the strike zone. If all couples had to go through such a process before they were allowed to have children, I believe that many would not qualify; a few might have second thoughts about starting a family. I am, of course, not advocating such an approach. My point is that parenting comes with significant responsibilities many would-be parents are neither aware of nor prepared for and, regrettably, some parents never learn to accept. With respect to education, one such parental responsibility is to make sure that children acquire a learning mindset so they are in a position to benefit from formal education and can see their inherent talent come to full bloom. Their gift might be beneath the horizon of parental recognition, but there is no excuse not to give children the gift of a learning mindset.

The children themselves are not off the hook either. Their responsibility lies in not squandering their learning mindset but to deploy it fully in the development of their natural talent. When someone has a gift that others might not have, that person has a responsibility to develop that gift. Nobody has the right to deprive society of the benefits that a fully developed talent could provide; anything less would be unfair and selfish. With access to formal education, which their talent development would benefit from, children have the responsibility to commit the learning mindset that their parents instilled in them. Hence, parents and their children both have responsibilities that are relevant to the educational process and that are important to the success of that process in cutting rough diamonds to reveal their natural sparkle. Next, to complete the picture, I will discuss the responsibilities formal education has in that process.

THE RESPONSIBILITIES OF EDUCATIONAL INSTITUTIONS

Beyond leveraging the learning mindset of students, what are the responsibilities of formal education? In line with my beliefs, I see three key responsibilities:

1. Identify the unique natural gift we all have, and do that as early as possible.
2. Match each unique natural gift with an educational program that can develop that gift to its full potential.
3. Do this in an affordable way.

We all have a gift waiting to be discovered and developed. My view is that the first thing formal education should be doing is to identify that gift and do this as early as possible. Unfortunately, we seem to be overconsumed with identifying deficiencies instead of focusing on the gift and the world of potential that gift contains. Just look at the ever-increasing list of learning disabilities and deficits! Those are all real and do deserve attention, but, as is the case with rough diamonds, we are all unique, and we all deserve attention. Even the smartest students I have worked with have special needs, not in the least the need to be challenged.

Formal education should be about special attention being given to the natural gift we all have and how that gift could be best developed. As with rough diamonds, focus should be on identifying potential first and then define the cut (educational program) that would reveal the inherent beauty the best. But this is not really what formal education does these days. We neither focus on identifying true potential nor on adapting the development of that potential to its nature and characteristics. We typically define a desired student profile and set minimum requirements for students to be admitted. We then proceed by developing whoever gets through the cookie cutter in pretty much the same, standard way irrespective of their unique potential.

To go back to the rough diamond analogy, this would be akin to defining a minimum profile a rough diamond should have and then proceed by cutting all the stones that pass the cut in exactly the same way. This is essentially what we do from grade one (and increasingly at younger ages as even pre-kindergartens are beginning to look more and more like formal schooling) all the way through higher education. We define a standard admission profile, cut out the lower tail, and proceed by educating those who passed the cut in a uniform way irrespective of their individually unique potential. And, note that the standard profile used to make the cut is typically set independent of the potential (and its variance) available in the pool of applicants. I will come back to this later in the book.

Ironically, when we look at how athletic (or artistic) programs operate, we see something much closer to what I believe education should be doing. For example, look at how a university such as LSU (last year's college football champions) recruits talent for their football squad: they scout for talent and when they find an athlete with a gift for football, they carefully craft it. This is more akin to what diamond cutters do in their trade. Hence, for all the hard-core academics who criticize universities for having extensive athletic programs, here is something their academic programs could learn from and adopt.

It is important to note also that we are pretty bad at identifying our own gift. Just because you like to do something, and you really want to do it, doesn't mean you are actually good at it. As an example, just watch a couple episodes of *X's Got Talent* (replacing X with the country or region you either feel part of or are curious about; the franchise pretty much covers most developed nations these days). Just as with rough diamonds, it takes knowledge and expertise to identify and recognize potential. I will let you judge for yourself if, in the case of these franchises, the judges actually have that.

Identifying potential talent is not an easy task. If, as I advocate, formal education should discover the unique gift we each have (and, when done so, craft an educational program that would bring out the gift's full potential), we need to define what knowledge and expertise is necessary to do that. Not doing it correctly or sticking with what we currently do has consequences. Missing a near-perfect rough diamond or cutting one the wrong way is costly in sparkle (and in cash!). Making similar mistakes with human talent is worse, as we all miss out. Just think of Susan Boyle.

Some might recognize the name and know her voice. Susan

was discovered on the show *Britain's Got Talent*. The You-Tube video of her first appearance on the show has been watched widely. I find the video revealing and educational. First, on how we miss out on true talent, and second, how human judgments focused on imperfections are blind to talent until we are rubbed into it with our noses (in Susan's case, our ears). Fortunately, Susan knew she had a talent and a passion to work on it. Her remarkable voice would have gone unnoticed if she had not been given a chance to appear on the show. She was 47 years old when she finally did. Just imagine the sparkle we could all have experienced had her gift been discovered at a much younger age. Her voice, herself, and all of us would have been so much richer. It makes me wonder how many Einsteins we have been (and are) missing out on. Let us not perpetuate an approach that leads to suboptimal results by missing out on near-perfect rough diamonds (and let us also stop glorifying cut glass).

Let me emphasize that education should be adapted to the unique gift we all possess. There is a lot of discussion around adaptive learning these days, but that discussion focuses on the cognitive learning profile of a student (i.e., his/her learning modality, speed of comprehension, emotional state, and adopted learning strategies). It is my belief that adaptation needs to go beyond just an individual's cognitive learning profile; it should also take into account the nature and characteristics of the natural gift each individual possesses. That gift is a rich world in its own and should be developed recognizing its unique character and potential.

When education is done in a social setting (as pretty much all formal education is done today), it should also be adapted to the mix of individuals in that social setting to maximize co-learning. As I will discuss later in the context of the MSM SKOLKOVO MBA, we engineered every class (i.e., selected qualified individuals in function of who we had already admitted and who would add a profile that would enrich the learning environment for all) and then adapted the program to the character of the class we had admitted. Although not easy to execute (because the program delivery becomes audience-dependent and, hence, dynamic), I do believe that such adaptation would result in much more efficient and effective learning. Let me digress for a minute and describe how my own teaching evolved over my academic career and became more adaptive to who was sitting in the classroom.

For those of you who might not have had the experience, teaching is not easy. It takes passion, effort, and dedication. With some nerve, most of us can walk up to the front of a classroom and read off teaching notes or presentation slides, but that is not teaching. Novice teachers pretty much all start out that way, and that is also how I initially taught. Sadly, many teachers and faculty never evolve beyond that.

Teaching is also not just storytelling. Storytelling is an effective communication technique in the tool kit of any seasoned teacher, but storytelling without proper framing and reflection will not result in much learning. For any audience to acquire knowledge intelligently, intellectual involvement and engagement are required. All the minds present have to be fully tuned in to the learning wavelength. And that is not easy to achieve, because everybody walks into the classroom with their minds who knows where. And those minds need to be roped in quickly. That requires building bridges to where those minds might be, which necessitates being in the know of your audience and what might occupy them at that moment. The pylons of these bridges are the credibility you have in the audience's eyes. That credibility comes from knowing your stuff but also from being able to project that into the students' world. Being able to give a perspective on where the knowledge to be conveyed fits into their world (and they can fit their world around it) is key to effective teaching. This requires the creation of a broad reference frame around the knowledge to be conveyed.

Prepping, which I still excessively do, used to be just memorizing a script but has evolved into creating that reference frame based on information acquired about the audience. Thus, the reference frame is fully adapted to the audience and defines the boundaries within which the script will be written collaboratively with the audience in real time.

The frame sets the limits within which to orchestrate the discussions so that all the shoes that need to drop do so. The frame gives everyone in the audience a structure with familiar anchor points from which their individual learning journeys can begin.

This collaborative teaching style is adaptive but only up to a certain point. It does not take into account each student's unique cognitive learning profile or the nature and character of their unique gift. My belief is that formal education should integrate those as well to arrive at fully adaptive education. Technology is likely to play a role in achieving this because it enables unobtrusive assessment of individual idiosyncrasies that are relevant to learning, and it can easily scale any adaptation in real time. I will discuss technology and the role it can play later in the book. For now, let me go back to formal education's core responsibilities and address the final one: formal education should be affordable.

The physical delivery model we most commonly identify formal education with is both labor intensive and physical-space intensive; it requires teachers (faculty), administrators, classrooms, office space, etc. Those all make education not only expensive but also inflexible and not easily or readily scalable. The financial burden is significant for governments (in public education) and for students and/or their parents (in private education). But there are ways to reduce that financial burden without jeopardizing the learning (and, perhaps, even enhance it). Consider the full-time MBA program we created at MSM SKOLKOVO.

The full-time MBA program we built at MSM SKOLKOVO was almost entirely experiential. The experiential learning vehicles were five field projects in three geographies (Russia, US, and China or India) and a startup project that could be anywhere in the world. The projects were selected carefully to make sure the required material was covered and the learning objectives were achieved. In each case, the leadership team had to be involved and only projects that were candidates for implementation were accepted. Impact was key to secure the right motivation from both the students and the companies and/or organizations we worked with. Unless there was such a motivation, learning would be compromised.

Two projects were in Russia: one with a private company and one with a government agency (federal or regional). In the US, the projects were with high-tech startups that experienced exponential growth challenges. A fourth project was with a local company either in China or in India. We shied away from multinationals as one of the objectives was to also learn about corporate culture in different cultural contexts. The final project was a startup, which students could develop further upon graduation (and many did, successfully). All projects were team projects with classmates except for the startup project, where the students were entirely free on who they worked with and brought into the project (i.e., they were not confined to just having classmates on the team).

The project work took about 15 months and was preceded by a three-month kickoff in Moscow. Those three months were typical course-type work that had as an objective the alignment of the students and the acquisition of a knowledge base needed before diving into the projects. Aligning the students was necessary because we maximized variance in the admissions process. For example, we had students who had worked as traders on Wall Street, but we also had students who had been artists. As I will come back to later, variance is an important basis for learning.

Furthermore, and in line with the mission of the school (which, as noted already, was to develop entrepreneurial leaders for difficult environments), we do not always have the option to assemble an A-team in difficult environments. We have to work with what is available and try to build an A-team. Maximizing variance in admissions also required us to build a unique learning process around the profile of each individual class. The whole approach was very adaptive and different for every incoming class. The only element we rigidly stuck to was our objective.

Apart from the startup, all projects had to be done in

teams. We created the teams to optimize the cross-learning potential and to adhere to our mission because in difficult environments we often have little choice in who we get to work with. In all of the teams, each student had an opportunity to lead his or her team and learn about leadership the hard way. The support infrastructure consisted of learning coaches, academic faculty, and senior partners in top consulting firms. Each student and each team had a professional learning coach. Faculty provided the foundation lectures, substantive lectures when project work required them, and academic assessment. The senior partners worked with the teams one day a week in their respective geographies. Their role was to supervise the project work, make sure that it moved along, and convey critical project management and project execution skills. These senior partners did all this for free. The incentive for them to get involved was that they really got to know some of the talent coming down the learning pipeline.

The companies and organizations that provided the projects paid all the costs directly related to the projects plus a modest fee. The total cost was well below what a leading consulting company would charge for a similar project. There was a win-win built into the approach: the client entities would get quality work at an extremely competitive price, and the fee paid by the client for that work would offset some of the tuition costs for the students. This is one way to alleviate the cost of education, but there are undoubtedly others that could be pursued.

Another obvious way to reduce the financial burden to students (and governments) is to integrate technology into the traditional delivery model. I will discuss the role that technology can play in education in detail later in the book. Let me illustrate here how it could be integrated to alleviate the cost of college education.

A college education (undergraduate degree) typically takes four years to complete. In most disciplines, the first two years are mostly foundation courses, many of which could easily be delivered online (and many are already). Why not put all those courses online, free for all? Students anywhere in the world could take the courses at their own pace and then commit to a rigorous assessment at the end to qualify for admission to the last two years on campus. Universities and colleges could lower the tuition cost for the on-campus years to complete the degree. As a win-win, this approach would have benefits for students and for colleges/universities. For students, it would bring some flexibility and lower the financial burden of a college education. For universities, if the drop in tuition is less than 50 percent of the tuition they currently charge, they would still gain financially in the tuition collected per admitted student. They would also benefit from a reduction in student recruitment costs, and they'd get better students (in talent and in motivation). In fact, many universities are realizing that MOOCs are effective student recruitment tools.

Consider, for example, top research universities such as MIT, Harvard, Stanford, etc. In their league, each cannot afford to miss out on a future Nobel laureate. Such talent is neither easy to scout for nor to spot. But with some advanced MOOCs and rigorous testing to go with them, unique talent could be identified in every corner of the world in a cost-effective way. All it takes is to view MOOCs in a different light: not only as delivering knowledge but also as a recruitment tool. College would become more affordable for many, and universities would be able to spot unique talent better (and, potentially, earlier) and align it for more effective engagement (and learning) when it comes to campus. This seems like a no-brainer to me. There are probably even better variants on this approach to tackle affordability within the current delivery model.

My concerns with the prevailing business model go deeper. When I look at the cost structure of formal education, I find that its nature makes education susceptible to dynamics that can easily steer it off course and chip away at its integrity. Let me explain.

The cost structure of the physical delivery model of formal education is fixed-costs heavy. That makes it susceptible to two dynamics we see in other high fixed-costs service industries: standardization in delivery and marginal cost appeal. Both are worrisome when we consider their consequences from the perspective of the core responsibilities of formal education. Standardization in delivery is exactly the opposite of the full adaptation formal education should strive for to secure effective and efficient learning. Marginal cost appeal makes educational institutions numbers-blind because adding a few students can bring much-needed revenues at virtually no extra cost. My view is that many educational institutions have overdosed on students as a result of this. They have become very busy beehives, which can be amusing to watch but hardly represent an environment conducive to learning. Recall the hummingbird feeder image I used when describing the MIT Sloan School cafeteria. I will dig deeper into these dynamics later in the book as they obscure a slippery slope that can put the integrity of education (and that of the institution providing it) easily and quickly at risk.

Taking the core responsibilities of formal education to heart, we need to seriously reflect on the prevailing model of formal education. That model is not readily amenable to cost-effective learning, to adaptative learning, and to lifelong learning. In fact, I will argue later in the book that we should develop a true lifelong learning paradigm first and then work back from there to reengineer formal education so that it can support that paradigm and secure adherence to the core responsibilities of formal education as I laid them out previously.

PUTTING THE INTEGRITY OF EDUCATION ON THE LINE

The tail end of my academic career was spent teaching undergraduate students at a top regional university in the Middle East. After years of being at the helm of business schools as dean, I was eager to go back into the trenches at the front line of formal education and work with young (and, hopefully, bright and eager) minds. I was also curious about what made the millennial generation tick and how technology shaped their world and molded their minds.

My students were pursuing a liberal arts degree in business similar to the very first students I taught years earlier while pursuing my PhD at Purdue University. Teaching while being a doctoral student was very much an exercise in keeping my head above water and barely succeeding. The focus then was exclusively on my own studies and not on those of my students. When I went back to teaching, I was much more interested in the students I worked with and in how I could contribute in meaningful and effective ways to their learning and growth.

Working closely with my students in the collaborative teaching style I had adopted (and described above), many showed a brightness and eagerness to learn. Whereas for others, I had doubts about their intellectual ability and mindset to pursue higher education. My crude assessment of their intellect was that a number of them did not have what it takes to be in college. No matter how much effort they put in, I did not see them being able to develop a significant level of critical thinking. Some of them really tried, and I admired the effort they put in, but universities are not there to certify effort no matter how commendable that is as a human trait. Probing into their mindsets revealed that talent was not the only thing lacking in some of my students. Given the general popularity of college education, I also began to suspect that I was not necessarily witnessing an isolated situation.

When I asked my students why they had come to the university for a college education, few could articulate a rational and coherent reason for doing so. Many even looked surprised at me raising the question. To them, it was obvious and the natural thing to do, and my question was silly and/ or naive. I will comment on what lurks behind this reaction shortly.

When I probed my students further on why they wanted to study business as opposed to one of the more traditional academic disciplines, I got a variety of answers. Some students revealed a genuine interest in business and expressed a well-articulated eagerness to learn the tools of the trade. They showed every indication that they had the learning mindset to benefit from a college education and succeed. Others gave answers that made me doubt whether they had such a mindset. Their answers ranged from picking business because they were not quite sure yet what to do with themselves and felt that business was broad enough to keep their options open to being channeled into business (in some cases against the will and desire of the student) as part of grooming them for a role in the family business. Although none expressed it explicitly, I also suspected that a few had taken a bet on business being an easy subject to bag a college degree. As I worked with my students, some of my fears panned out, and it was clear that besides those lacking the intellect to be in college, others lacked the necessary mindset to be there.

This situation raised a number of questions in my mind. Admitting unqualified students must have consequences. What might these be? How did such a situation come about in the first place? What could give rise to what I observed? Perhaps college is a window onto a slippery slope that any educational program could fall victim to.

One of the consequences of admitting unqualified students is that academic integrity is challenged immediately. Given the profile of my students, I was not surprised to see some trample all over norms and values we hold dear in the academic world. That plagiarism, cheating on tests and exams, outsourcing class assignments, etc. were rampant is in part a result of the situation created by admitting unqualified students. Blame can be laid at the feet of the students, but it is the educational institutions that created the context and conditions for such behavior to blossom.

A more problematic consequence is the risk that the education of all the students gets compromised. There is a real threat of this occurring because students and faculty might adjust their behaviors as a result of the context they find themselves in. Unless they are truly self-motivated and understand what is unfolding around them, qualified students get the wrong benchmarks and might begin to slack in drive, motivation, and ultimately performance. In short, there is a risk that the situation chews away at the learning mindset of the better students. A few bad apples can spoil the bin.

Faculty might also adjust their behavior and regrettably in ways that would further adversely affect the quality of the education provided. The fact is that good students bring out the best in faculty and vice versa. But that powerful feedback mechanism is short-circuited as soon as a noticeable number of students are neither qualified nor motivated to be there.

Furthermore, as faculty typically target their delivery at the modal value of competence present in the class, they might lower that level to accommodate the unqualified students. That downward adjustment will affect everyone in the class. Also, by lowering the modal value, it moves away from the competence level of the best students in the class who, as a result, might no longer feel challenged. Faculty might also become demotivated, go on autopilot, and become oblivious to who is actually sitting in the class. As teaching has to come from the heart to be effective, this might spark a downward spiral in the quality of delivery.

In sum, the presence of unqualified students can have consequences that negatively affect the education of all and quickly put the integrity of education (and that of the institutions providing it) at risk. Most of my students did graduate despite my concerns about the qualifications of some of them, and it underscores that risk and could further undermine the trust in education and in the institutions providing it.

Taking a step back to reflect on how the situation I observed might have come about, it appears that there are dynamics at play that could easily give rise to it and that should raise a warning flag. As I personally observed, college is already susceptible to them, but other programs could fall victim to them as well. The dynamics operate on both the supply side and the demand side for students and can quickly lead to an overdosing on students with the fear that unqualified candidates might join the student population with consequences as just described. Let me explore the dynamics I see at play in college education.

On the supply side, parents feed the demand for college education. We have created a society where many parents believe that they have failed as parents if their kids do not make it to college. This is wrong. College (and university in general) requires an intellectual ability that not all children have. A lack of that ability does not imply a lack of any ability. In fact, as I articulated earlier, quite the opposite is true. We are all rough diamonds that just need a different cut to sparkle. With the right cut, we can all sparkle.

With current parental beliefs, some will do anything to get their kids into college. We recently witnessed a high-profile university admission scandal in the US: fraudulent behavior with parents and university administrators colluding to get essentially unqualified children into elite universities. The case gave rise to the term "bulldozer parents": parents who move obstacles out of their children's way. This behavior is so wrong at many levels, not in the least in parental roles and responsibilities. From experience, let me also add that the bulldozer behavior by parents (and others in their sphere of influence) does not stop at admission. Let's face it, if the children are not up to the task, their parents will have to clear their path all the way to graduation (and most likely beyond).

None of this will make up for the lack of necessary talent. Parents might do well to reflect on the rough diamond analogy: one can only appreciate the potential of a stone by holding it up to the light and looking at it from all angles. For the children themselves, nothing is more exhilarating and motivating than to discover that they are actually good at something and that they do have a gift to develop and share.

On the demand side, educational institutions have some thinking to do as well. As I discussed previously, the prevailing business model that higher education has adopted is numbers-hungry, especially when tuition income is a significant source of revenues. Tweaking admission standards to serve short-term financial needs would open the door to what I observed and, as a result, potentially undermine the education of all. As such, educational institutions that are driven by their business model might quickly and easily put their reputation and that of their educational programs on the line. It is indeed a slippery slope.

As the college example and its consequences make clear, access to any educational program should not be an unconditional right for all. Relevant potential and a learning mindset are necessary requirements to preserve the integrity of any education. Educational institutions would do well assessing those diligently. Parents would do well recognizing that their children are rough diamonds that require and deserve a unique cut to sparkle like no other.

CHAPTER FOUR

An Education for the Future

Formal education has basically not changed much in decades. We have become accustomed to the system and don't ask too many questions. The concern has mostly been in keeping it going so it doesn't go off the rails. Just look at how, in the aftermath of the Covid-19 pandemic, educational institutions are scrambling to grasp at any strand to hold on to the past.

INTRODUCTION

As with many things, we get used to a certain pattern and that becomes part of the normal. We develop a blindness to what is happening in front of our eyes. Therein lies a danger in that the rails formal education runs on might not be leading to where we would like them to go. As we've already seen, dynamics are at play that might push the whole system off course. Accordingly, it makes a lot of sense to take a step back and look at where we are and how we got there. That can only help us as we rethink the delivery model and the business model. Such reflection might point us to new models that are better aligned with the emerging reality and the need for lifelong learning.

In somewhat of a random order, I will reflect on seven aspects of formal education as we know it: variance, distance, outsourcing of responsibilities, habitat, model, content, and technology. My reflections are meant to stimulate creative thoughts about how we should educate future generations.

VARIANCE

Throughout my academic career, I moved around the world and had the opportunity to experience and learn about many different cultures. Every place I went to, I tried to learn the local language. One reason was to show respect to the local people and their culture, and every culture deserves respect. The other reason was that in the process of acquiring a language, one learns quite a bit about the culture that speaks that language. A language is very much a window into the soul of a culture.

One thing I rarely did was hang out with fellow expats. In

fact, I never really went to my embassy or consulate unless I really had to (as for getting a new passport). This is not always a smart thing to do as I found out in Beijing in June of 1989. As was the case with many foreigners, I was trying to get out of China. When I reached out to my embassy for assistance, I found out that everybody had already left the country!

I am proud of my small home country, and I try to visit it as much as I can, but when I decide to work on the other side of the world, my home roots are very long. When I went to China, I wanted to learn about China, and the only way to do that was to hang out with Chinese. If I wanted to hang out with fellow countrymen, I should have stayed home. After all, there are many more of them there and I was bound to find a few I could get along with.

What would I learn from hanging out with expats in China? Probably reinforced (and mostly negative) stereotypes of the culture I was keen on getting to know better. Just go to any expat bar anywhere in the world and listen to the conversations: pretty much all complaints and jokes about the "weird" locals. I didn't really want to get my mind peppered with negative stereotypes. I have always been a person who likes to check the source and not just rely on somebody else's judgment and/or interpretation.

My eagerness to learn required me to spend time with the

locals, people not like me but different from me. It was in that difference that the learning was hiding. If I spend my time hanging out with fellow countrymen (people very much like me), what was I going to learn? All learning finds its origin in differences or what statisticians call variance. When we see differences, we naturally question: why, how much, where, etc. Looking at variance is like looking through a window; looking at fellow countrymen would be looking into a mirror.

Note also that by looking at others who are different from us, we also learn quite a bit about ourselves. If we all eat with chopsticks, we don't question why. That question never comes up. But when all your life you ate with a fork and a knife and now you are surrounded by Chinese eating with chopsticks, questions pop up. Why did I learn to eat with a fork and a knife? How did that evolve? And so on. Looking at variance makes a learning mind very inquisitive and reflective.

Most of us learn about variance in statistics classes. Looking at data, we typically use two summary statistics: mean and variance. The mean gives us insight into the central tendency in the data. It is often the only statistic we work with. But as we learn in statistics, that summary statistic is meaningless unless we also look at the variance. Variance captures how the data is dispersed around the mean. As the variance in the data increases, we have more data points away from the mean and, hence, the mean becomes less representative of that data. It is the variance that gives meaning to the mean. As any data scientist knows, the information is in the variance; that is where the secrets are hidden. The quest to uncover those secrets captures the learning that is inherent in variance.

Small children seem to know this. It is as if we are all born being natural data scientists, but we lose that skill as we grow up. Small children rarely play with others of the same age. That is until schooling conditions them to do so. When they have the choice, kids generally prefer to play with older children because they instinctively know they can learn from older kids. Young kids know that variance is a source of learning and a benefit to them.

Note also that when we look for role models, we never really look for somebody who is the mirror image of us. We look for somebody different but somebody whom we admire, can learn from, and get inspired by. We look for meaning-ful variance.

Thinking is exploring variance: no variance, no thought; no thought, no learning. This begs the question why formal education largely shuns variance and does not leverage it in the learning process. For example, I have often wondered why it is that we do all our formal schooling with children of the same age. We all start out when we are about seven years old with grade one (or local equivalent) and move with same-aged cohorts all the way through college. And why? How much are we going to learn from people who are exactly like us? But that is what we are doing in formal education. We're cutting down on variance, the bedrock of learning. Harvard Business School admits about 900 new MBA students every academic year. In the admissions process, they all go through the same cookie cutter. The net result is a class profile with a high average but with small variance. Why do we do this? I can only come up with one answer: convenience. The pedagogical model we have adopted does not like variance. In that model, variance is a headache and not an opportunity. It seems to me that we are missing out on something fundamental. How did this happen?

When admitting students at all levels, educational institutions use admission criteria that collectively define the profile of the student they would like to admit. That profile is the cookie cutter, and any applicant who goes through it gets in. That common approach cuts down on variance, some of which might be useful and could even be leveraged in the learning process.

When I introduced the project-based MBA we created at MSM SKOLKOVO earlier in the book, I mentioned that we maximized variance in the admissions process, which is the opposite of what typically happens. Clearly, basic talent and potential had to be there, but beyond that we went for very different profiles and engineered each class in such a way that we could adapt the pedagogical process to maximize the learning for all. It required an adaptive and highly flexible approach, the opposite of the industrial-factory model that characterizes formal education. We did not want to create echo chambers but groups with inherent variances that were meaningful to explore and exploit in the learning process. Every student was there to learn but also contributed in meaningful ways to everyone's learning.

In the entrepreneurial context we were trying to create, we also felt that variance would be a useful source of creativity if leveraged properly. It creates challenges, but we felt all these were important opportunities to learn from and make the pedagogical process richer and better.

The predominant delivery model we use in formal education today does not handle variance well, even though it would be to the benefit of all students. Teachers (and faculty) do not like variance in the classroom as it makes traditional teaching difficult. The comfort zone of most teachers is a narrow variance around the mean (i.e., a class with no fat tails). Hence, it seems that we have traded variance for convenience. But convenience is never a good reason to do anything, not at least in a context where learning is pursued.

Have we created an educational model that is afraid of

learning? The current delivery model gravitates toward standardization to secure operational efficiency, and a steady flow of student numbers keeps the machine well oiled. While understandable and predictable, this is a move away from learning and from building intelligence into the system. Contrast that with machine learning, a popular topic in artificial intelligence (AI) today.

How do neural networks learn? They essentially do so by looking at variance in huge data sets. A facial recognition algorithm cannot learn to recognize faces by looking at one face, even if it looks at that face a million times. The algorithm learns by looking at millions and millions of different faces. Deep learning in AI is dissecting pixel data at multiple levels and learning from local variance across pictures. These numeric AI approaches thrive on variance, and all the intelligence it builds artificially is extracted from variance—variance across any picture and not just those that went through a cookie cutter. An interesting observation to reflect on is that machine learning capitalizes on variance as much as it can while traditional education promotes learning by cutting down on variance!

To be fair, variance is not totally absent in traditional education. Many educational institutions support diversity in gender, race, etc., and they should. Diversity is variance, but it is seldom motivated by the learning opportunity it provides. Unfortunately, diversity is typically motivated by political arguments. The variance implied by diversity is hardly ever used or leveraged in the pedagogical process. It helps with photo ops in brochures and on websites, but that is where it stops. In my view, this is a truly missed learning opportunity.

Variance is an opportunity waiting to be explored and exploited. But not just any variance. In the context of learning, I make a distinction between negative and positive variance. Positive variance is variance that benefits learning; it is the variance small children instinctively look for. Negative variance is variance that can undermine learning. For example, admitting unqualified students increases variance in the talent pool in a class, but such variance will adversely affect the education of everyone, since all actors in the system will adjust their contribution to levels away from what education should really deliver.

We need to bring positive variance into the pedagogical process and leverage it fully. We need to recognize that variance might be dynamic and that it could change over time. Accordingly, how that variance is best integrated in the learning process will change as well. As we engineered each MBA class at MSM SKOLKOVO based on the positive variance in the applicant pool, we ended up with a different class each year that provided unique opportunities to leverage the variance represented in it. We simply could not just standardize the approach year in, year out if we wanted to maximize the co-learning potential.

DISTANCE

All through high school, I spent my evenings in a small art academy in my hometown. I have always enjoyed drawing and painting and feel I have some talent in that department. My parents always thought I would grow up to be a painter; I guess I have not grown up yet! I see my gift as a combination of a good eye, a sense for structure and balance, and a feel for colors. As a gift or raw talent, it is a whole world, and in my case, one that is still waiting to be fully discovered. My interest in and curiosity about the beauty and exactness of math got me sidetracked, and my artistic talents remain dormant for now. As many of us do, I keep thinking of going back to painting when I retire (whenever that will be!).

In my formative years at the art academy, I had the great fortune of working with a locally well-known painter. Although I did not know or understand it at that time, that experience was a unique deep dive into the true process of learning. The experience was truly exhilarating and transformational. He was not a great teacher in the traditional sense of being able to communicate and explain things well, but he was a great educator in his own way. He did not teach me much about paint, pencils, and drawing techniques; the education was way beyond that. To him, the mechanics of drawing and painting were just a sideshow. His focus was on sensing and feeling art, sensing and feeling the subject one was going to draw or paint. It was a holistic immersion involving body, mind, and soul, and not just an exercise for the hands. I remember vividly that we were not allowed to touch pen, paper, or canvas until we had fully immersed ourselves into the scene that we were going to paint. He helped us truly experience art with all our senses, and that was the learning. Only a painter who has his or her heart and soul into artistic creation and expression can do that in a powerful and motivating way. Just focusing on techniques and mechanics is learning without depth. The passion he brought to opening his world to me was transformational, not just transactional. I did not realize it at that time how precious that experience was and the profound impact it had on me.

Looking back, that experience illustrates an important ingredient of a true learning process, one we have largely lost in formal education. Formal education has over time created more and more distance between the creation of knowledge and the dissemination of that knowledge, depriving students of the wonder and passion of creation, exploration, and discovery. The artistic energy and passion the painter brought to my art class enabled me to acquire the full power of creative expression, not just the technical skills to paint and draw. There is a true loss in keeping a student at a distance from the source of knowledge. As the chess grandmaster Kasparov writes in his book *Deep Thinking*, he can tell who trained playing chess on a computer.

When we go back into history, and this is the case across cultures, the writers, thinkers, philosophers, and scientists of the time were the teachers. Students in those days could literally touch these great minds, and those teachers touched the students like no one else could. The creator and inventor of knowledge was the teacher. In their teaching, they not only revealed the knowledge they had arrived at but they also shared how they had gotten there and why; that context gives a much better and deeper understanding of the knowledge that was being conveyed. Learning is itself a process of discovery, and being able to align that with the process the creator of the knowledge followed brings learning to a whole different level.

We rarely see this in formal education today as most teachers (and faculty) deliver content they acquired but did not create. Many of them don't even know the origin of it or in what context it was developed and created. The content is no longer tethered to its creator(s) and its origins. In fact, when we step back and look at formal education, we see a machine of messengers who repackage and translate the knowledge they acquired somewhere else. There is a loss in this, a loss that takes some of the flavor out of learning. Just listening to and learning from a creator of knowledge is not the same as listening to and learning from a messenger. There is (are) human(s) at the source of all knowledge. The source is never a book, a video, or a post. Over time, we seem to have moved further and further away from the source as we lay more and more tracks between the source and the student. To me, that adversely affects the quality of learning and the depth we can master in the knowledge being conveyed.

Most teachers (and faculty) are just knowledge messengers. Some are good at this. To be effective at it, they have to be good. However, a creator doesn't necessarily have to be good at it. The painter I worked with was not a great teacher, but by putting his body, mind, and soul into his profession, it made him the best educator. In my view, if the knowledge is not part of you, and you have not lived it (or live it), it is difficult to make an audience acquire it. Let me describe an episode from my academic career to make the point clearer.

Lifetime employment is very rare these days, except in the academic world where many universities (all of the top ones) still hold on to the tenure system. Tenure secures lifetime employment for qualified faculty. The qualification criteria vary across institutions but typically cover research productivity, teaching, and service to the community. In top research universities, research productivity receives almost all the weight in tenure decisions.

In general, it is not easy to get tenure, and there is quite a bit of prestige attached to being a tenured faculty at a top university. There is a lot to be said about the tenure system, but much of it is not relevant for the discussion here. Suffice it to say that from a management perspective, tenure is an expensive exercise as it essentially converts variable costs into fixed costs. I already commented earlier on what happens in complex service delivery systems with high fixed costs. To be honest, as a faculty member, I appreciated tenure; as a dean, I did not. (I was a tenured academic until I gave up tenure to become the Founding Co-dean of MSM SKOLKOVO in Moscow.)

When the university where I spent the tail end of my academic career proposed instigating a tenure system, I was more than puzzled. I could understand some faculty pushing for it, but I could not understand the university leadership offering it. When faculty were consulted on the proposal, I noticed that one of the first faculty who wholeheartedly supported the university's proposal was the leading human resources (HR) faculty in the business school. This dumbfounded me. I am not an HR specialist, but I couldn't think of a model or rationale in modern HR thinking that would justify lifelong employment. Here was a colleague teaching one thing and living another. What that faculty taught was disconnected from what that faculty believed in. This concerned me a great deal as I don't believe that anyone can be an effective teacher unless they truly believe in what they teach. That is partly why creators of knowledge, even when they are not perfect communicators, are so effective in inspiring curiosity and in stimulating learning at a level well beyond what the typical messenger-teacher can achieve.

Exposing students at all ages to passion in the learning process is important. Passion in a subject matter and passion in conveying that subject matter stimulates learning because it is contagious; it ignites curiosity and motivates learning. The creators of knowledge do this naturally because of their intimate involvement in and with the knowledge they created. They are typically also eager to talk about it and share it. Teachers (faculty) who are removed from the knowledge source can still bring passion to their teaching, but it is not quite the same as what the creators bring to the dissemination of their knowledge. Any dissemination of knowledge without passion results in just a dry and dull delivery. As students might quip, "I might as well read the book myself!" Young children are especially sensitive to passion (as they are to all kinds of emotions). Passion is inviting and fans their eagerness to know more and learn. We need to capitalize on that more in education. Let me convey a story to make my point.

Last summer, I took my six-year-old daughter to an outdoor market in the French countryside. It was in a small town and local farmers were selling their produce. A traditional blacksmith had set up shop in a corner of the marketplace, where he happily hammered away around an open fire. He was clearly in his own world, enjoying what he was doing. My daughter was fascinated and just watched with full attention to every move the blacksmith made. She initially stood at a distance absorbing the scene but then moved slowly closer and closer until she was right next to the blacksmith. This was a whole new experience for her and it clearly captivated her. Children are always fascinated by new things and are eager to discover and learn, if given the chance.

The blacksmith didn't have much of an audience beyond my daughter; the locals were all sitting in the middle of the town square chatting and drinking wine over a meal. The blacksmith was quite passionate about his craft and just worked away in the last sunrays of the day. Noticing my daughter approaching, he started talking to her about what he was doing. And my daughter's avalanche of questions started rolling. As all kids captivated by somebody doing something novel, she wanted to have a go at it herself. It is as if children have a natural understanding that the best way to learn is to try it yourself. Of course, she went for the blacksmith's biggest hammer, which she could not lift! The passion displayed in the novel setting was all it took for her to get immersed.

Young children have a natural disposition to learn. As I will discuss later in the book, we as humans are born discoverers: curious, eager to explore, ready to learn. I am not sure we fully capitalize on that in formal education. Children can also read emotions and people very well. They can sense when somebody is passionate about what they are doing even though they have no clue what that means and what that unleashes in them. But it does set them on a path of wonder, curiosity, and learning. Passion truly ignites and lubricates a learning mind.

The fact that most teachers (faculty) are merely messengers of knowledge raises questions about their role, if any, in the pedagogical process going forward. Today, most knowledge is widely available and readily accessible, and the days that teachers (faculty) were an important (and often the only) source of knowledge are long gone. In fact, students in class today have access online to the very information the teacher is conveying to them and can (and often do) check in real time whether what they are being told is true. Indeed, the credibility of any teacher can be lost quickly in the information age.

The question then arises whether there are more effective ways to convey knowledge that do not involve teachers (faculty) or where they would play a different role. Recall the project-based MBA program we created at MSM SKOLKOVO where faculty's role was confined to three activities: teaching some basic knowledge to ground and align students upon their entry into the program, the performance assessment of the students, and the design of the projects (i.e., making sure that the required knowledge in each functional area was properly addressed in the project work). The project management itself was put in the hands of seasoned professionals with deep knowledge of the geographies where the projects were being executed.

Experiential learning, of which project-based leasing is just one format, is a powerful alternative to standard classroom teaching. There is also gamified learning, where knowledge is conveyed using games that can simulate real-life scenarios. After all, airline pilots are trained (continuously) on flight simulators, so why not adopt that approach in formal education?

I became familiar with computer simulation games as a powerful tool in education when I was a faculty member at INSEAD. The first business simulation game, MARK-STRAT, was developed there almost 40 years ago. Indeed, and contrary to what some might believe, gamified learning is not exactly new. I used that game and others many times over the years and became a big believer in the power and potential of gamified learning. But it has to be done correctly. That means with close but unobtrusive supervision, constant feedback, and adequate time for reflection. Again, and a fundamental requirement to me, learning does not occur unless you take time to reflect. Letting any group of students (at all ages) loose on a game without those necessary ingredients leads to gaming; all they learn is how to game the game. That is the fundamental challenge to gamified learning. Nobody questions the power of games in stimulating motivation and sharpening focus. Because of this, they are a tool to be leveraged more than we do today, but with the understanding that we play to learn and not learn to play!

Computer-based simulations lift the cover off technology and the role it could play in the pedagogical process. As I will discuss later in the book, we have not even begun to embrace what technology is increasingly capable of. Distance might provide the opening it needs to fully deploy its capabilities in the pedagogy of future generations.

OUTSOURCING OF RESPONSIBILITIES

As children grow up, their parents are generally responsible for their behavior. We would expect parents to monitor (with the help and input from educational institutions) the effort and dedication the children bring to their education. Communication between the frontline people actively engaged with the children and the parents is crucial in this regard, especially at younger ages. But it is ultimately the parents who should hold their children accountable. This requires parents to be parents, but many aren't. My impression is that some believe they can just outsource all their parental responsibilities to educational institutions. Although educational institutions play an important monitoring role, it is not their responsibility to discipline behavior. They can set rules for what is required and acceptable behavior in school, but beyond that, the parents should hold their children accountable. Let me describe a unique educational program where technology monitors the children's behavior and progress in their learning journey.

The founder of MSM SKOLKOVO is of Armenian descent, and through him I got to know the TUMO Center for Creative Technologies. TUMO is a fascinating educational project in Yerevan, Armenia. It was created (and financed) by a US entrepreneur of Armenian descent. The project focuses on teaching children (7–18 years old) creative technologies. The education runs parallel to day-to-day schooling with children coming in the evenings and on weekends. The program is open to all and is entirely free. Children sign up and each of them becomes an avatar in an online, onsite learning system. The school building is an open space where each child sits at a custom-designed computer desk that can move around throughout the open space. There are no teachers and, except for a few graduates from the program who provide help and backup support, the whole educational process is run and monitored intelligently online. As children progress through their adaptive learning journey, they can share creative ideas and/or achievements on central monitors for all to see. As part of their learning journey, they attend movie sessions, online gaming activities, and some dedicated classes where they work collaboratively on specific projects. In a play on variance, none of these projects are done by age cohort. When I first visited the project years ago, one group of children was working on recording the music for a Hollywood cartoon production, and another group was working on programming the fountain in the park where TUMO is located in central Yerevan.

The whole approach TUMO adopts to learning creative technologies is quite different from traditional education and illustrates what education could be (or, perhaps, should be). As I have often observed (and to some extent was involved in myself), true innovation in education seldom happens at top educational institutions. It happens in distant corners all over the world. After my first visit, I showed my colleagues the short video that I had recorded at TUMO and asked them where they thought this project was taking place. None mentioned Armenia. The video shows kids of all ages glued to their screens in an atmosphere full of positive energy. For me, the experience was amazing and I felt that perhaps I was looking at the future of education.

The children come to the TUMO center anytime they can outside of normal school hours. Their learning journeys are entirely adapted to the talents they exhibit, and they differ across students. They are not on any fixed schedule, but they have to show progress in their learning journey.

If they do not show progress or come to the center infrequently, they get kicked out and cannot come back. This is how the intelligent system monitors their progress, and they are held accountable with a heavy stick. That stick is obviously a deterrent, but the dedication I saw the children bringing to their learning journeys avoided its frequent use. That dedication appeared to come from two key characteristics of the learning process. First, they learned quickly that they could actually do something unique and creative. They discovered that they had a gift, and that was both motivating and inspiring. Second, they could see the progress they were making as their avatar moved through an adaptive learning cycle. Accordingly, they saw that their efforts and dedication paid off.

An intelligent system recognizes what each child is good at and drives him/her further into that direction, weaving a magic carpet that takes the child on an incredible learning journey. The contrast with formal education could not be more startling. Important for our discussion here is that the learning system makes the children responsible and holds them accountable for their progress and learning. I know of no parents who hold as heavy a stick as the TUMO learning system does. Perhaps they should.

Who is holding the parents accountable? Their responsibility is to instill a learning mindset in their children. Some do; many don't. In fact, I believe that many parents feel they can just outsource this responsibility to the formal education sector. They see their role as confined to getting their children into good schools. As the university admissions scandal I referred to earlier suggests, some bulldozer parents see no limit to achieving that. For many parents, anything beyond getting their children in is the responsibility of the schools.

My feeling is that children should arrive at school with a learning mindset, and educational institutions would do well assessing that they do (and also keep track of that mindset as children go through their education). It is the parents' responsibility to instill that learning mindset in their children, and that responsibility cannot be outsourced. But who is holding parents accountable for that? We really have some reflection to do on being parents and the role we play in the education of our children.

Who is holding educational institutions accountable? In higher education, many of these institutions teach about the importance of holding people accountable, but do they actually practice what they preach? Who is currently holding them accountable and for what? Educational institutions worry about their reputations and invest heavily to protect and strengthen those. But reputation is a broad and vague concept. The many rankings that exist for higher education, for example, capture a broad range of indicators, but none seem to relate directly to the core responsibilities these educational institutions have. As discussed, those responsibilities are to identify the gift (potential) each student has and then develop that gift to the fullest in an affordable way. I know of no ranking that actually assesses students for the incremental impact an educational program had on the development of their unique talent. That delta (i.e., the difference between raw talent on arrival and the development level achieved upon graduation) would be a good measure to obtain on the way to developing a student's inherent potential. Of the wide range of criteria the rankings of academic institutions are based on, none assess that delta. It is also missing from the accreditation requirements of academic institutions. These requirements merely assess process issues and, as such, provide useful benchmarks for new institutions building educational programs. They do miss out on assessing whether educational institutions live up to the core responsibilities they have, and that makes it difficult to hold them accountable.

With true accountability lacking, what are the consequences? A focus on the reputation of the institution and not on the students' learning. In fact, learning has been outsourced to the students. It has become the students' responsibility. If the student is truly motivated to learn, he/she will learn. But the reality is that in many educational programs today, students can muddle through without much learning. Given the consequences of admitting unqualified students, many don't learn much except how to beat the system (and, from experience, there is no limit on creativity there). It requires a lot of self-discipline for qualified students to truly develop their inherent talent in the current system of formal education.

To achieve accountability, more resources should be devoted to assessment, particularly unobtrusive assessment of talent enhancement. I believe that we should move away from relative assessments and develop methods that are imbedded in the learning process and that can assess actual talent enhancement (i.e., the delta). With such assessment would come an ability to hold educational institutions accountable for their core responsibilities. That accountability would anchor them and safeguard the integrity of the education they provide. It would also enable educational processes to become more intelligent, something they currently are not. In a crude way, we could think of education as a manufacturing process. In the age of intelligent manufacturing, it is perplexing to see that the education of students of all ages is not managed in any intelligent way.

HABITAT

Buildings are designed and built with a specific purpose in mind. The outside (the shell) typically functions as a billboard to communicate an identity, vision, and/or ambition; i.e., the architecture is supposed to make a statement.

Just think of the Guggenheim Museum building in New York (US), a Frank Lloyd Wright design, or the Guggenheim Museum building in Bilbao (Spain), a Frank Gehry design, or the Bank of China building in Hong Kong, an I.M. Pei design.

In contrast to the outside, the interior design and layout are created to align with an envisioned use. That is why airport terminals look and feel very different from museums. Just think of the prominence and prevalence of signage in the former as opposed to in the latter. I generally don't need my reading glasses running through an airport, but I do in pretty much every museum in the world. Even the large, wall-covering Rubens paintings in the Louvre in Paris carry small-lettered tags that blend into the color of the walls!

The design of the inside and the outside are not independent from one another with the design of one putting restrictions on the design of the other. Because of this, there are two basic approaches that can be followed when designing a new building: one is to design it from the outside in (i.e., the shell becomes the defining parameter); the other is to design it from the inside out (i.e., the interior design becomes the defining parameter). A lot of thought goes into which approach to follow and how to actually design the inside and the outside. Once a building is built, it will reveal what those behind its design had in mind. School buildings are no exception to this. Their designs reveal how those behind them view education.

Over my academic career, I was involved in the design and building of two new business school buildings: CEIBS in Shanghai (China) and MSM SKOLKOVO in Moscow (Russia). The two were totally different experiences. The CEIBS campus was designed from the inside out, and the characteristics imbedded in the phase one design have been preserved in two major expansions built over the last 25 years. The MSM SKOLKOVO building was designed from the outside in. Its footprint is a typical avant-garde Malevich design representing the school's Russian roots and its ambition to be ahead of its time. The single-building shell is an incredible architectural piece designed by David Adjay. As with any outside-in design, the engineering requirements to build that shell ate up quite a few degrees of freedom for the interior design. We had to design classrooms and work spaces around the many pillars that supported the giant glass disc. But large open spaces compensated for the classroom design challenges. Ironically, some of those challenges forced us to think creatively about the design of classrooms and work spaces and, as such, became sources of innovation.

For the design of phase one of the CEIBS campus in Shanghai, I brought in Pei Cobb Freed and Partners. They had just finished building the Anderson School of Management at

UCLA and knew what a business school was, how it operated, and perhaps more importantly, how business school people think. The design parameters for the shell were a minimalist design, a Chinese touch (the Suzhou tiles that became the defining characteristic of the campus buildings), and the vision of a global knowledge center. To achieve the latter, the library building became the anchor structure of the campus—a cube floating in a black marble pool. The architecture is not as imposing as the MSM SKOLKOVO building (even with the signature I.M. Pei-type glass pyramid integrated in the phase three expansion), but the focus and emphasis on interior-space layout and the atmosphere it creates gives the campus a serene feeling. Even when many students are on campus (and there are many!), it never gives the feeling of a busy beehive like so many other schools and universities do (especially the urban ones). The CEIBS campus remains an oasis of monastic-like tranquility conducive to thought and reflection.

For an environment to be conducive to learning, the energy and atmosphere it radiates are important. A school building is not an airport or train station, which are places that derive their energy from their natural busyness. A school building should derive its energy from the mind-opening serenity that well-designed museum buildings have. A building that derives energy from people feels empty (and ghostly) after hours. That emptiness is as disturbing to the mind as busyness can be. Learning requires reflection, and reflection requires a mind that is at ease so it can tune into deep thought. A school building that feels like a busy train station is not conducive to thought and reflection. It might enable efficient knowledge delivery, but you have to flee the place to reflect on what has been delivered in it.

I love to sit in an old church or a monastery, and while there, I often read a book or just think. I never really went and sat in a classroom after hours. Well, I did a few times, otherwise I wouldn't be able to share the feeling! Classrooms feel dead late at night and early in the morning. The purpose for which they were designed makes them that way. It is worth taking a step back and looking at the typical design of a classroom and the atmosphere that arises from that design.

The classroom has become the core and defining feature of our educational infrastructure. We all have spent quite a bit of time in them during our schooling days. For those who are teachers or faculty, we spent most of our professional lives in them as well. The classroom is the frontline infrastructure; whatever form or shape it takes, that is where the rubber meets the road. It is the physical context where teachers (faculty) convey their knowledge to students who typically sit quietly in a prearranged and fixed pattern. Its design has evolved over time from rectangular-shaped flat rooms to multitiered amphitheaters. Whatever the form, they all share one defining characteristic: classrooms are designed to secure undivided attention to the teacher (and today, his/her screen). In that way, they are truly teacher-centric. Undivided attention is increasingly secured by making classrooms windowless. In many business schools today, amphitheaters are built into the ground with no natural light (and if there are any windows, thick curtains will almost certainly block it). Students are forced to focus on the teacher and immerse themselves into the teacher's world.

When entering a classroom, students are expected to leave reality (and their world) at the door. They enter a sanitized world defined and controlled exclusively by the teacher. That world is not always the one in which the knowledge to be conveyed was created (or should be applied), but it is the one the teacher feels comfortable in. In that sanitized world, it is the teacher who decides when, how, and what other reality can enter into the world he or she has created. Students can bring in their world of experience, but under tight control by the teacher. The tightness of that grip is determined by the depth of knowledge and the comfort and confidence the teacher has with that knowledge. The teacher is the master of ceremony and in charge. This also explains why many schools (and faculty) prohibit students bringing any technology into the classroom that is connected to the outside world. Some even block Wi-Fi signals going into the classrooms! This perhaps benefits some faculty, but I am hard-pressed to see the benefit for the students. Should we be educating future generations in a reality that is divorced from the one they live in and will have to function in?

The link between reality and education needs some reflection. In higher education, for example, what are the consequences on learning if the ivory-tower mentality is still prevalent in academics? Blocking reality risks alienating students, which then might undermine the undivided attention classrooms were supposed to create. I also believe that learning in a vacuum limits the depth of that learning. Context is important. That is also why I raised the concept of distance. Unless the faculty is the creator of the knowledge to be conveyed, the delivery will be devoid of the context in which it was created, and that limits the depth of learning. How we educate today resembles the running of a controlled experiment, but one where we focus much more on the control than on the outcome.

Reflecting on the importance of bringing reality into the learning process, I have often wondered what would happen if reality was brought into a school. At one point in my career as business school dean, I wanted to have a real trading floor inside the school building (instead of a digital ticker tape running in the cafeteria); i.e., allow a bank to place part of its trading team in the school. I also thought about consulting companies (and others) having a working office in the school. For sure, this introduces questions and challenges, especially if we take the perspective of the traditional delivery model. If you take a step back, think how this could be integrated into more novel learning models with students at the center. There are so many ways we could enrich the knowledge delivery and the learning process. In fact, I believe that more learning would be achieved if delivery was cast in the context of the reality we are actually preparing the students for.

We also need to truly flip the classroom and put the student at the center of the educational process. The focus in formal education should be on effective learning and not on efficient delivery. The student and his/her potential should be the focus with teachers (faculty) being tools who in a coordinated and targeted fashion develop that potential to the fullest. Going back to a crude analogy I already used, I know of no manufacturing process where the focus is on a tool used in the process and not on what is sitting on the production line!

Formal education should not demand undivided attention from the student, but it should secure undivided attention on the student. One step in the direction of a flipped classroom would be to make the classroom truly interactive. When I was dean at MSM SKOLKOVO, I wanted to create a classroom where all the walls were unobtrusive screens and where any device that was in the classroom could project its screen anywhere onto the walls. Whoever was in the classroom could enlarge, zoom in on and/or move around the projected screens. The idea was to stimulate collaborative learning and have the students' screens, as opposed to the teacher's screen, anchor the learning process.

No doubt, there are other ways to configure physical spaces that would put students at the center and be more conducive to their learning. As I wrote in the introduction to the book, I spent time in the entrepreneurial ecosystem around the university while on sabbatical at MIT. I observed a lot of learning going on in the incubators, accelerators, and coworking spaces. In fact, I came to view these spaces as co-learning spaces. People just sat around in relaxed settings and discussed, questioned, and reflected together. As the setting takes the edge off the unnatural feeling of a classroom, I wondered how we could emulate these co-learning spaces in school settings. The more real and relaxed a place feels, the more conducive it is to learning, and the more spontaneous that learning becomes. As busy beehives, you have to flee most schools these days to be able to think, reflect, and learn. As the delivery model has become more numbers-driven, we have created distance between the initial exposure to knowledge and the absorption of that knowledge. That is not what I observed in the co-learning spaces as exposure, thought, and reflection occurred simultaneously. You could see the light bulbs going on right there! We should let these spaces inspire us instead of getting further absorbed into the hyperdesign of the traditional classroom.

Taking a step back, there is of course the question of what physical spaces, if any, will be needed in formal education in the future. And that future has gotten a lot closer all of a sudden. As all crises do, the COVID-19 pandemic has accelerated history. The lockdowns we all experienced led to school closures and a massive move to online teaching. Online is undoubtedly part of the future, but not in the format the pandemic catapulted schools into. Online teaching is classroom teaching done online with the teacher still being the center, but with the students at a distance from the teacher and from each other. All are just tuning in without being there in person (but hopefully in mind). It is the old delivery model put online. As with education in general, online education will have to evolve from delivery to learning in line with the core responsibilities as described earlier.

As a cautionary note, there is really no such thing as online learning, and we should perhaps refrain from using the term. There is online exposure to knowledge that might lead to learning. Learning requires thought and reflection, something no online platform can do for us. We have to put our minds to it.

Online and offline will have to be stitched together into a new paradigm that stimulates and enhances thought, reflection, and learning. If done well, it can shorten the distance between the exposure to knowledge and the learning of that knowledge. For all the challenges the pandemic crisis created, it has given us an opportunity to roll up our sleeves and get to work. We should not waste much time on using online platforms to save the old model (and our past). We should emerge with a new model for the future. Physical contact will always be part of the pedagogical process, but we need to reflect on when, where, how, and for what purpose. I doubt we will find much use for traditional classrooms. Inspired by what I saw in entrepreneurial ecosystems, informal co-learning spaces are probably a better model to aim for, and indeed, improve upon.

MODEL

As with many things we become accustomed to over time, we often do not notice how they have evolved and what defining form they have slowly morphed into. Furthermore, when reference points are lacking or are not readily available, we become blind to what is in front of us: the hidden-in-plain-sight syndrome. This is the case with formal education. We know it and accept it for what it is, but we do not really take a step back to reflect on where we are and whether that is where we should be. I want to do just that and focus on three characteristics of what formal education has become. First, formal education is largely confined to the early stages of our life with uninterrupted schooling that then forms a foundation for a career (or careers). Second, formal education is a standardized delivery service resembling the industrial-factory model. Third, formal education is built around bundling knowledge. Let us explore each of these characteristics and reflect on them in the context of the emerging reality and the core responsibilities I ascribed to educational institutions earlier.

THE ALL-THEN-NOTHING MODEL

The legal schooling age differs by country, but children typically start with grade one (or the local equivalent) when they are six or seven years old and graduate from college when they are 22 years old (or one or two years older if they take a gap year between high school and college). For most of us, that was our journey: 16 years of mostly uninterrupted formal education. If the retirement age is 65, we roughly have about twice that amount of time for a professional career (or multiple careers). That is the "all-then-nothing" model: all formal education upfront, mostly uninterrupted, followed by a career (or careers) for about twice the length of time we spent in school. Some of us might stop our career(s) or go straight through after college to get more advanced degrees. Others will at different points in time get additional training that's necessary (or required) for career advancement. For most people, however, the sequential model of "all-then-nothing" characterizes where formal education fits into their life's journey. Let us reflect on this in the context of the emerging reality I described earlier in the book.

The reality in most industrialized nations today is that the life expectancy continues to increase, and we can all look forward to living longer than our grandparents did. Because of aging populations in many of these nations, retirement ages have been creeping up as well. We might all live longer, but we are also likely to have to work longer. At the same time, rapid advances and innovation in many fields drive knowledge creation at an ever-increasing pace. This implies that in the fields where such advances occur, knowledge gets outdated more rapidly. Thus, the period of time we have to put what we learned in school to productive use is shrinking if we do not stay abreast of the advances being made. Accordingly, we will be expected to work longer at a time when we might get outdated faster. This interplay challenges the continued viability of the sequential "all-then-nothing" model of formal education. Clearly, we have to get very serious about lifelong learning.

As I will discuss later in the book, lifelong learning is not about going to school longer and piling up more degrees. It should be thought of as a continuous process of building and enhancing capabilities that enable versatile deployment of those capabilities, and where those deployments (i.e., careers) themselves become an integral part of a never-ending learning journey. This will require fundamental changes in how we think (and feel) about formal education, in what formal education actually consists of and does, and in how we deliver that education. In this new paradigm, formal education can no longer be seen as a chore, a rite of passage, or something we have to do and put up with. It will have to be seen as something we want to do and look forward to doing.

Novel business models will need to make lifelong learning affordable. Just stretching the current model of formal education out over one's lifetime would make education prohibitively expensive. I believe that the sequential "all-then-nothing" model has run its course and needs to be revisited.

THE INDUSTRIAL-FACTORY MODEL

Formal education has very much adopted the industrial-factory model: standardized curricula, standardized timing, and a standardized pace. Once a student has picked a school, discipline, and degree, he/she knows the length of the program, the speed at which he/she will move through the program, and what the curriculum will be like. All those are determined externally and independent of the student's cognitive learning profile and/or the character of his/her talent and the potential that talent might possess. We very much educate future generations at all levels and ages the way we put a car together on an assembly line. We just don't kick the tires when they come off the production line (on occasion, I would have liked to!). Formal education has become a machine running on autopilot with everything set up for efficient delivery to a large number of students, which the prevailing business model requires to stay afloat. This makes a highly structured, regimented, and rigid system focused on delivery and not on learning.

The analogy to car assembly stirs another thought about where this industrial-factory model might be headed. If you have been in a modern car assembly plant, you have seen the industrial robots at work, 24/7. Recall that most teachers (faculty) are just messengers of knowledge they neither created nor own. In the current approach to formal education, they are easily replaceable by technology. With truly intelligent (AI-powered) robots on the horizon, technology might be able to do better. Standardization drives the current system, but it might ultimately also be its demise. That is exactly the origin of the disruption that so many industries have fallen victim to. So, why should formal education be any different?

Before digging deeper into the industrial-factory model characterizing formal education today, let me contrast it to how a sports prodigy is coached to bring out the full potential of his/her natural talent. We can pick pretty much any sport, but let me look at tennis.

In the end, all tennis players play the same game according to the same rules. But they all develop a unique style, which turns strong elements of their natural talent into potent weapons for the game. The development process involves a dedicated team of experts (coaches, doctors, physiotherapists, etc.) focused on the prodigy, whose talent is identified as early as possible. At the center is the prodigy, and everything evolves around fully understanding, developing, and capitalizing on all aspects of the prodigy's natural talent. No prodigy is the same, no talent is the same, and no development program is the same.

This is the polar opposite of what formal education has become in terms of developing intellectual ability. Just imagine what would happen if we developed tennis prodigies using an industrial-factory model! We probably wouldn't know Roger Federer or Rafael Nadal, and I doubt that many of us would be interested in watching a tennis match. The beauty of the game lies in the fully adaptive development of rare but extraordinary talent. Why should intellectual talent be any different? A brain is not that different from a leg or an arm muscle. It is perhaps more complex, but that complexity might also harbor a richer and more diverse potential to be discovered, tapped into, and developed.

What makes formal education fit the industrial-factory model? The standardization in curricula, timing, and pace (at all levels and all ages) gives rise to a one-size-fits-all model. Once in a program, the curriculum is the same for all students. For example, there are different high school systems around the world, but within each, what subjects are covered and when they are covered is fixed and not adapted at all to any of the students' unique profiles. In college, curricula differ by discipline, but within each discipline, the curriculum is fixed. Some colleges and universities run honors programs for the better-performing students, but that is the extent of adaptation to a student's potential. No program takes into account the cognitive learning profile and/or the character of the intellectual talent each student has. And none take into account the mix of talent represented in the class.

In higher education, most curricula have a core of required courses that each student has to take. Beyond these core courses, electives are offered, and the student can choose which ones to take to fill out his/her program. Some students seek advice on which electives to take, but generally the choice comes down to what the student likes and not what he/she would benefit from. Referencing chocolate (unless you are Belgian), what you like is not necessarily good for you! Few if any programs provide students with advice on what would benefit them in light of their intellectual ability and potential. It is not only across students that curricula are fixed. In many instances, they do not change much over time either. I already mentioned this being the case with the MBA curriculum in business schools.

Why do curricula change so little over time? Both internal and external reasons contribute to the lack of change.

Externally, regulations and accreditation play a role in that certification often requires sanctioned curricula. Internally, in established institutions, curriculum discussions get political quickly. In the case of MBA programs, most business schools have a curriculum review committee. As a faculty member, that is about the last committee one wants to be on. The reason is that most start out with lofty ideas but quickly turn into turf fights because of the resource implications. The curriculum is a zero-sum game and, hence, if you want to put in something new, then something old has to be dropped to make room for it. As faculty lines and other resources are typically allocated on the basis of a department's contribution to the curriculum, departments will fight any attempt to have one or more of their courses dropped. Accordingly, even though curricula should be determined by demand, they tend to be determined more by supply. The cart does get before the horses very quickly in curriculum discussions.

Standardization of the industrial-factory model characterizing formal education goes well beyond curricula. Length and pace are standardized as well. For example, primary education is six years, secondary education is six years, college is four years, etc. That is why we all have pretty much the same number of years of formal schooling irrespective of our intellectual ability and/or cognitive learning profile. Looking back at the years I was teaching undergraduate students, the best of them did not need four years to acquire critical thinking skills. By the same token, not all of us are fast learners. Some of us would benefit from a slower pace to get to the full potential of our ability. In sum, much more flexibility and adaptation is needed as it would benefit us all.

Besides the standardization in curricula, timing, and pace, there is another aspect of the adopted model that should be pointed out as it directly affects the depth and quality of learning. That aspect is the lack of a pause button. Once in an educational program (and it is pretty much the case for any program), we find ourselves on its conveyor belt being fed knowledge at a steady pace. There is no option to temporarily stop the conveyor belt, step back and take time to think and reflect. As I have already pointed out, learning (and especially true deep learning where knowledge is digested and absorbed) requires much thought and reflection. To enable that, we need to stop and take a step back from what we are doing.

Throughout my career, I have taken time off to think and reflect. Let me illustrate what I do to make that a valuable learning exercise. When I left the deanship at MSM SKOLKOVO, I took a year off and spent it at my home in the French countryside. I felt a need to write about my experiences in Russia. There was no ambition to write a book, but writing helps in structuring thoughts and sharpening focus. I started by rereading all the great Russian literary works from Nabokov to Tolstoy. Prior to moving to Moscow,

I had read some in the hope of discovering (and understanding) the Russian soul. My thinking was that after my experience, rereading these works would help me understand better what had happened to me there and bring me closer to grasping what the Russian soul was all about. I felt that the great Russian novels would provide valuable scaffolding when I started dissecting my experiences and learning from them.

In academics, we have a wonderful opportunity to hit the pause button in what is called a sabbatical. Depending on the number of years of service, a faculty member can take half or a full year off for just thinking. In fact, one gets paid to do it just so one can concentrate on thinking (instead of doing). For most, we just go to another institution and that is what I did at MIT in the Spring of 2017. Being off-radar and off-grid with no deadlines and/or responsibilities gave me ample time to think and reflect. Taking time to rewind and reflect on knowledge acquired and experiences lived promotes inquisitive intelligence and deepens learning. I came to appreciate the concept of a sabbatical, and I see it now as an integral part of the process to stimulate and grow intellectual curiosity. As I will write later, this is core to true lifelong learning. As such, a true sabbatical is a pause button that should not be a privilege for academics only.

But what are the consequences of the rigid system of formal education we have in place now? Standardization in formal education helps efficient delivery but almost certainly leads to suboptimal talent development. In my academic career, I have come across quite a few extraordinary people. I am not just referring to the many accomplished scholars whom I got to know and work with. On occasion, I ran into some whose potential I thought was underdeveloped; they seemed to have an intellectual capability that went well beyond what they relied on and worked with. I could see an intellectual fuse that never got lit. I never confronted them with this observation, but I did feel sad. As an educator, you could not feel any other way. What a shame, I thought, particularly since we are more accustomed to seeing people who think they have more than they actually do.

The question we should raise is: in our pursuit of efficiency, did we miss the next Einstein? We will never really know, but chances are that we might have and that some extraordinary talent either remained dormant (undiscovered) or did not get developed to its full potential. If that were the case, it would be a loss not only to the individual involved but potentially also to society at large. To make this first consequence a bit sharper, the standardization we see in formal education would be akin to cutting all rough diamonds exactly the same way irrespective of their potential. Indeed, a brilliant way to ruin brilliance.

A second consequence is that a lack of adaptation leads to an educational system where smart students (the upper tail in the distribution of intellect) remain unchallenged. Unless they have a learning mindset and the motivation to push themselves, their true potential might never emerge. The danger is that the industrial-factory model of formal education, which does not address their special needs, begins to chew away at their learning mindset; i.e., good students getting bored and/or demotivated. This might be accelerated when unqualified students surround them.

A third consequence of the one-size-fits-all industrial-factory model is that by ignoring variance across students, it cannot be exploited. The model runs on autopilot and does not seek ways to learn and improve itself. That makes it devoid of any intelligence. The result is that we educate future generations in a system that is anchored and frozen in the past.

I believe that many of us are aware of these consequences and that the dubious opinion some of us have about formal education finds its origin in somehow knowing (or suspecting) these consequences. We can and ought to do much better. My belief is in dialing the clock all the way back to formal education's core responsibilities and develop a new model that addresses those responsibilities and holds formal education accountable for them.

BUNDLING KNOWLEDGE

A third characteristic of the model that formal education has morphed into is the bundling of knowledge into degrees, the basic unit of formal education. The curriculum of any degree defines what the bundle consists of for that degree. That bundling is then mapped into textbooks and other educational materials for that degree.

When we start our schooling with grade one (or local equivalent), we follow a fixed curriculum, and it is pretty much that way all through high school (at least within the same high school system); i.e., one standard and fixed bundle of knowledge for all students. In higher education (i.e., college and beyond), those bundles of knowledge become less diverse, but students have a choice of which one to pursue. The bundles are typically structured around a core discipline that identifies the degree's concentration. At younger ages, the bundles are diverse and cover a broad range of subjects deemed necessary to convey at that age. No subject is tackled in any great depth. Accordingly, the motto early on is breadth over depth. That balance reverses as we move into higher education where breadth is traded for more depth in the selected discipline.

The discipline forms the knowledge anchor of the bundle, and other subject matter that provides intellectual scaffolding for that discipline is added to round out the bundle. If, for example, you select biology as your subject of concentration, and you pursue a degree in biology, you will get exposed to all aspects of biology as well as any other discipline or subject matter that provides support and/or enhances the understanding of biology. Accordingly, the core discipline (biology) functions as a gravitational force in the knowledge bundle. Before reflecting on the implications of this bundling, let me take a step back and discuss what makes an area of study (or subject matter) an academic discipline. The reason this is important will become clear momentarily.

Not all disciplines are considered academic disciplines. The two characteristics that will make it so are rigor and theory. Rigor characterizes the process by which the discipline's knowledge was created. If proven methods of scientific inquiry were used to build the knowledge base, then the academic standards of rigor were respected. Such scientific inquiry typically requires extensive exploration and probing of empirical observations to establish undeniable facts. Theory goes beyond those facts (or empirical observations). It consists of a conceptual but comprehensive framing of knowledge supported by the observed facts. Where scientific inquiry discovers facts, theory builds knowledge by extrapolating beyond those facts. For academic purists, any discipline that is steeped in rigor and theory is considered an academic discipline. Accordingly, the bar is high and it takes a long time for a discipline to earn the label "academic."

My interest here is not in making judgments about which discipline deserves to be called academic and which one does not. The reason I made this little detour is that, in my view, exposure to and understanding of rigor and theory are important in the learning process. This will especially be the case as we leave the sequential model of "all-then-nothing" behind and integrate formal education into a new paradigm for true lifelong learning. Both rigor and theory form the foundation and the scaffolding of critical thinking. In that regard, I believe that getting a good and fundamental grounding in a traditional academic discipline is warranted. That is why, despite having been a business school dean, I never felt comfortable about an undergraduate degree in business.

My discomfort comes from business not really being an academic discipline. It is an applied field that borrows from a wide range of academic disciplines, i.e., from economics and statistics on the quantitative side, all the way to psychology and sociology on the behavioral side. Jumping into a field without a good theoretical grounding in any of its underlying disciplines seems reckless to me. It would be akin to having a surgeon cutting away without a profound knowledge and understanding of human biology. There is a reason why medical students go through rigorous training in chemistry and biology before launching into medicine. Theoretical grounding provides depth, perspective, and a solid foundation to build on. In that regard, I felt (and still do) that an undergraduate degree in business is like erecting a building with no foundation to support it. I believe that a good grounding in a basic academic discipline will become all the more essential with true lifelong learning looming on the horizon. Such grounding unleashes an intellectual capability that bears fruit well beyond the discipline of focus. Indeed, it strengthens the mind.

Going back to the bundling of knowledge in formal education, what are the consequences of such bundling? There are two. First, bundling around a discipline creates a gravitational force toward the center of that discipline. In other words, the knowledge is anchored at the heart of the discipline that becomes the center of focus. This is not where innovation and creativity typically occur. Those occur at the edges, often where one discipline touches another or even begins to overlap with another. Bundling might draw attention away from fertile ground for discovery and progress.

A second consequence is that bundling prevents intellectual wandering across disciplines, something I consider important in developing perspective and insight in any particular discipline. Such wandering constitutes another example of variance benefiting learning. These two consequences suggest that we might want to rethink the bundling we have adopted in formal education. As I will argue later in the book, if bundling is warranted, it should not be based on a discipline but on the talent each of us possesses.

To recap, the current model of formal education has three characteristics: an all-then-nothing structure, industrial-factory standardization, and knowledge bundling. All three have consequences that question its future viability as we refocus on the core responsibilities of formal education and create a new paradigm for lifelong learning. In my view, a radically new model is needed. However, radical change might not be easy to accomplish. First, even if most of us agree that change is long overdue, few would advocate a radical change. In situations like this, most people gravitate toward a practical change. I am all for practical, but never at the stage of defining the objective of change. Focusing on practical considerations at that stage tends to cast a long shadow over creativity. If those considerations color the starting point, irrespective of the lofty ideas that might have prevailed at the outset, one will end up with only marginal changes on the existing model. Such changes would result only in digging a deeper hole to fall into.

Radical change is starting with a clean sheet of paper, a mindset disconnected from the past, and an undivided focus on what should be. For me, practical considerations should come in only when we have to decide on how we get from where we are to where we should be. In other words, the practical comes into play at the execution stage and not at the design stage. Practical considerations play a role only when we look for a path from where we are to where we should go. Like walking through any maze, no matter how complex it is, there always will be at least one path to get from the start to the finish (and back).

Regulations (and accreditations) will hamper change as well. Formal education is inundated with regulations. Some regulations are necessary to avoid abuse and to secure conformity. However, as with any regulation, we tend to overshoot and overdo it. It's my belief that we have definitely done so in formal education. The problem with regulations is that they tend to be anchored in the past and give rise to bureaucratic processes that stifle experimentation and innovation. Accordingly, they are rigid and promote rigidity. They do not evolve and nail the whole system in place. To put this in perspective, let me explain what we faced at the creation of CEIBS and how we dealt with it.

When we were negotiating the creation of CEIBS, the Chinese educational authorities (in those days, the State Education Commission) told us that we would not get our degree officially recognized unless we followed a sanctioned curriculum. That curriculum required, among other things, the study of Marxist-Leninist Thought. I just could not see myself going to Brussels and asking the EU to invest in a new business school teaching Marxist-Leninist Thought; that was clearly a nonstarter. To give a proper context to this, CEIBS is legally structured as a 50/50 JV between the EU and the Chinese government. Each side is represented by an executing partner. On the EU side, that partner is the EFMD, which is based in Brussels, and on the Chinese side, that partner is Jiao Tong University in Shanghai.

To cut a long story short, we did not get the degree approved because we stuck to a curriculum we thought would benefit the talent China needed for its rapidly changing economy. We didn't really care that much because our focus was on the students, their education, and their placement. Our thinking was that if we placed our students well, this market recognition might force the hand of the Chinese authorities. After all, if it did not, they would lose all credibility. And that is exactly what happened. In fact, a lot of CEIBS' success lies in focusing on what mattered: a demand-driven quality education. Focusing on regulatory requirements leads us to take our eyes off the ball. To be honest, I can't think of any project that turned out to be successful and that started with bureaucratic blinders.

In rethinking the model of formal education, it is important to clearly define the core responsibilities of formal education as I did above. Given those responsibilities and the need for lifelong learning, we need a radically new model— one that is intelligent and adaptive, and one that is woven into our life's journey and is not a ritual or a rite of passage to it.

CONTENT

What we learn in school depends very much on what is conveyed in the classes we take. When we take a class in trigonometry, for example, we are exposed to the field of trigonometry and will learn something about trigonometry. I want to reflect on the content that is conveyed in the context of the emerging reality as described above. But first, let me discuss the delivery itself because what we learn in school not only depends on the content delivered but also on *how* that content is delivered. I already revealed this earlier in the book when describing my introduction to creative expression working with a known painter. Different delivery approaches of the same content do not lead to the same type of learning.

Consider the following two scenarios on how to become a better cook. One is to take a cooking class where you learn how to prepare various dishes: what ingredients to use, how much of each to use, when and how to combine them, etc. You take the class together with other aspiring cooks, each standing at an individual cooking station. At the end, you eat each other's dishes and the teacher comments on the prepared dishes. This class follows what I will call the recipe approach to cooking. You basically learn how to execute specific cooking tasks (e.g., how to bake artisan bread, how to make a chocolate soufflé, etc.).

Contrast this scenario with one where you shadow a

renowned cook. You go with the cook to the farmers' market early in the morning to see what is in season. The cook introduces you to what is freshly available and how each available vegetable could potentially be used. Next, you walk over to the local butcher and do the same. You explore the different cuts of meat, consider what looks good and fresh, and how some of those cuts could be combined with the selected vegetables from the farmers' market. Based on what you find, you create a meal together. With the shopping done, you set off for the kitchen to prepare the meal together. This scenario is more a bottom-up approach where you first learn about ingredients and how they could be combined into an appetizing meal before preparing that meal. The focus is not just on the mechanics of cooking but also on visualizing what is possible given the ingredients on offer.

Both scenarios will help you become a better cook, but what is exactly learned and at what depth differs greatly. The recipe approach comes down to learning how to execute a set formula. The bottom-up approach teaches how to create a formula given constraints on ingredients, and then execute that formula. The recipe approach is about learning a sequence of steps and what to do at each step. You essentially develop a mechanical knack for cooking. There is little creativity and reflection involved. Beyond making mental notes of what is needed and the sequence of execution, no thoughts are stimulated.

In the bottom-up approach, the mechanics are second-ary and follow a creative process involving thought and reflection on what could be done with what is available. In other words, you develop a deeper understanding of the full complexity and the art of cooking. That understanding is neither required nor revealed in a recipe approach. The mechanics of cooking the meal, and the focus of the recipe approach will naturally flow out of the deeper understand-ing of ingredients and how they can be combined.

Which of the two scenarios would you enjoy? Which one is more transactional, and which one is more transforma-tional? Which one of the two scenarios resembles formal education more? It is perhaps difficult to generalize, and there might be hybrids of the two delivery models in use. Pondering the last question, let me reflect on what I have seen as a worrying trend in business schools. I suspect that other practical disciplines might witness the same trend.

For pretty much every discipline taught in business school, I have seen a trend toward distilling knowledge into reci-pes and then teaching those recipes in class. Knowledge is conveyed in the form of problems, and then recipes are introduced on how to solve those problems. Let me put my cards on the table (and this should not be a surprise to many of you by now). I am not a big fan of this approach. To me, learning recipes is not learning at all. Recall that the set objective of higher education is to stimulate critical thinking; i.e., thinking with a critical mind. Matching problems with recipes requires little of that.

Let me also put that observation in the context of the emerging threat of artificial intelligence (AI). If a discipline's knowledge can be distilled into recipes, intelligent agents can be trained to do these tasks at least as well as humans. I am a big believer of the collaborative role of AI with human intelligence. But for that, we need to develop human intelligence in areas where AI falls short and not in areas where AI's strength lies. Intelligent systems, no matter their level of sophistication, cannot and do not think. Human thought is truly unique. Accordingly, if knowledge is distilled in recipes and delivery comes down to teaching recipes, we are diluting and weakening the very thought processes and capabilities we as humans will need in the age of what Satya Nadella, Microsoft's CEO, calls ambient intelligence.

Focusing specifically on the content of what we cover in formal education, let me frame my reflections in the context of two pertinent characteristics of our times. First, we all have access to infinite amounts of information in real time. Some of that information is factual, some of it is pure fiction, and most of it is part fact and part fiction. Second, we live in a time of persistent change at an ever-increasing pace. What does "relevant" mean in the context of such rapid change? Let me reflect on the content we convey in education, anchoring my thoughts in that reality of infinite access to information and rapid change.

The days that teachers, the local library, and the home encyclopedia were the main sources of information are long gone. As we are all plugged in pretty much 24/7, we continuously wade through masses of information online. Most of that information is unedited and unverified, and in many cases contradictory. In the online world, everybody seems to be an expert on something. More importantly, an opinion and a factual statement are largely indistinguishable for most of us. This situation will only become worse as we become more and more addicted to the constant access.

Understanding that addiction, I adapted my own teaching by switching away from my screen to the students' screens. In fact, I no longer use slides or PowerPoint presentations. With the infinite access online, I tell my students (and myself) that the best slides, the best videos, the best case studies, or whatever I need is already out there. In the collaborative teaching style I have adopted, I have my students find what I need. As I described earlier, when I asked my students to look for specific info (the example I used was the market cap of Apple), they invariably came up with different numbers. Few, if any, had any sense of how to probe those numbers and assess which one, if any, might be the correct one. Students lack in info literacy as they are not equipped to separate fact from fiction. In fact, not only students take anything they read online at face value. Many people forget that most online platforms are just unfiltered channels and are not the source of anything that gets posted on them. A good dose of critical thinking is required to distinguish fact from fiction. In higher education where the objective is to develop critical thinking, we are in the bizarre situation that we need some of it to develop it. Information overflow got us into a catch-22!

At the very least, this situation requires formal education to include info literacy in curricula as early as possible. Source credibility, convergent validity, false equivalency, etc. are critical notions we need to understand to secure factual learning. Scientific discovery follows a rigorous process to uncover facts and truths. Developing info literacy is parallel to understanding the tools and processes of scientific discovery. That is one of the reasons why I argued above (and will come back to later) that a good grounding in a traditional academic discipline is so crucial. Such training would equip students with valuable thought processes they need to become intelligent users of unfiltered online content.

There is also another element of real-time information access creeping into teaching (and beyond): the threat of instant credibility checks. Any factual statement a teacher makes can (and will) be instantly verified. With most teachers just being messengers of knowledge, they better be real-time informed about the true state of affairs in their field. The concept of distance combined with instant access to information creates a reality where the credibility of anybody making any statement can and will be instantly challenged. Just look at any news site today and the media's love for fact-checking. Unfortunately, few, if any, of these sites educate the public on how to fact-check. To me, formal education has the fundamental responsibility to do so. Perhaps there is some silver lining in students being able to hold teachers accountable in real time for what they are saying. More accountability is needed to anchor education and protect its integrity and our trust in it. I already alluded to this need, and I will discuss it in greater detail later in the book.

The other point to reflect on is the impact of rapid change on the content we teach. Foundation knowledge is perhaps timeless and context-independent and is not much affected by change. Disciplines that evolve rapidly, however, face the challenge to deliver knowledge that is up-to-date. If the faculty (teachers) are also the knowledge creators, they are most likely aware of the changes because they are part of the process of change. Most faculty (teachers), though, are merely messengers. For them, the challenge is to bridge the gap between them and the knowledge source in real time.

In general, formal education does not directly assess whether the knowledge delivered in the classroom is up-to-date. Whether it is depends very much on the motivation of the faculty (teachers) themselves. The only people who can hold faculty (teachers) accountable are the students through their real-time information access. Indeed, quality control is outsourced to the students! We can now understand why some faculty (teachers) prefer their students don't have internet access in the classroom. In fact, when I look back on the many faculty I worked with as a business school dean, it was the ones who were making the effort to stay current who didn't mind stepping into the students' world.

Is just-in-time delivery enough? It is not, and the reason for that lies in education being a lead sector. We in education pride ourselves on the fact that we educate future generations. And we really do. But with that comes the responsibility to equip them as well as we can for the future that they are likely to encounter. If we teach today what people need today, we are just addressing deficiencies in education. We should have taught them that knowledge in the past so they could be fully operational today.

Just look at the explosion of soft skills in business school curricula (and especially their popularity in executive education). Consider how much time and effort goes into leadership development at a time when we witness a serious drought in true leadership across the full spectrum of society (politics, business, etc.). Just scan any newscast any day of the week and you'll discover the majority of stories came down to a lack of leadership in one way or another. Better late than never, but we do need to recognize that all these efforts are remedial and are the result of deficiencies in the timing of our delivery.

The problem is that these remedial efforts can easily perpetuate themselves because we start looking at the future through a rearview mirror. Demand for these remedial efforts can quickly crowd out any thought about what leaders might need in the future and should learn about today. I worry that we do not truly address those future needs. Let me share some thoughts on this to illustrate the more predictive or anticipatory thinking that formal education as a lead sector should adopt.

How do we best prepare corporate leaders for tomorrow? What should we be teaching them today so that they would be fully equipped for whatever the future might hold in store for them? Of course, the first question that pops up is what will that future be like. I don't have a crystal ball (well, I do, but all I see is a crystal ball), but there is one characteristic I am willing to bet on. The future is likely to be one of continued disruption, i.e., perpetual change that will keep all of us off balance. The context in which we will experience such perpetual disruption will be one of ambient intelligence, i.e., a world where we are surrounded by smart devices and intelligent agents. I see a world where ambient intelligence will empower us while environmental dynamics will challenge us. The questions we need to ask ourselves are: what role, if any, will human intelligence play in that kind of a world? And what does this imply for the development of human intelligence in education today?

As we are already beginning to see, AI will play a major role in our lives. Leading a company with AI at one's fingertips will enable collaborative decision-making where intelligent devices act as virtual colleagues. I believe this will require corporate leaders to develop a capability to supplement and, if necessary, supplant AI in real time. To visualize such a collaborative effort and help us understand the competencies needed in such efforts, envision the cockpit crew in a modern airliner.

Various systems feed the pilot and the flight engineer intelligence in real time. When the airliner hits a pocket of turbulence, they need to quickly assess whether to disengage the autopilot and take control of the aircraft. An unpredictable event forces them to escalate from a monitoring role to a decision-making role that instantaneously requires their full attention, depth of expertise, and creativity on how to handle the new situation. Where the intelligent systems do all the flying and take all the rationally optimized actions under normal flight conditions, the event might force these systems outside of their "data comfort" zones (i.e., the data realities which they were designed for and trained on) and require the crew to think quickly and act decisively. This is what collaborative decision-making with AI-empowered agents (or devices) might look like in a managerial context.

I could well imagine senior managers having multiple intelligent devices on their executive teams enabling them, as the cockpit crew, to monitor and assess continuously and, when required, make decisions instantaneously. Ambient intelligence will enable corporate leaders to do these tasks and be decision-ready wherever they are and whenever they want. Such an empowering but decision-intensive environment will require some capabilities that in my view are not emphasized in managerial talent development today. It also points to capabilities that might become secondary or obsolete as intelligent systems will already have them and could easily outperform humans when deployed.

To properly equip corporate leaders for tomorrow, I see three areas where talent development needs to be enhanced: (a) "last mile" focus, (b) harnessing "fast and frugal" heuristics, and (c) stimulating imagination. Let me explore each in some detail.

LAST MILE FOCUS

The curricula of business schools are generally more content-intensive than decision-intensive. A lot of time is spent on concepts, taxonomies, and models. In the language of Bloom's learning taxonomy, these imply lower levels of cognitive activity as opposed to higher-order learning, which focuses on mastering thought processes to critically and creatively solve problems. In other words, a lot more time is spent on building the scaffolding than on using that scaffolding to actually build something.

In the future I envision, the core role of corporate leaders will be real-time decision-making using inputs from intelligent devices. Available at one's fingertips anywhere anytime, these devices will do all the rational and logical "thinking" fast and, within their data comfort zones, flawlessly. Senior managers will need the intelligence to act decisively in real time when confronted with unpredictable situations. To develop that intelligence, a shift in emphasis from content-intensive to decision-intensive learning is needed.

HARNESSING FAST AND FRUGAL HEURISTICS

As intuition is the operating system of efficient thinking, speedy decision-making will require the honing of intuitive intelligence. Very little if any attention is devoted to that in business schools today. There is far more emphasis on developing the rational mind than there is on developing the intuitive mind. The situation is actually worse because the over-emphasis on rationality has given intuition and heuristics somewhat of a bad name. We have come to accept that rational analysis is always right and intuition is suspect. This is the core tenet of behavioral economics, which is very well described in Daniel Kahneman's book *Think Fast and Slow.*

My view is that AI systems will do the slow "thinking," but they will do that very fast. What decision makers will need to complement that ability is the intuition to *act* fast intelligently. That will include an intuitive assessment of whether the rational and logical "slow" embedded in the AI system is valid; i.e., whether the reality faced is within the AI system's data comfort zone. In my view, talent development should focus on nurturing intelligent intuition or the acquisition of intelligent heuristics that make the fast near-optimal for the reality at hand.

Note that expert judgment is generally of an intuitive nature, and we should focus on developing and honing that capability. Let us remind ourselves of a quote attributed to Einstein: "The intuitive mind is a sacred gift and the rational mind a faithful servant. We have created a society that honors the servant and has forgotten the gift."

STIMULATING IMAGINATION

Human intelligence will have to step in where AI systems are bound to fail, i.e., beyond data and beyond criteria-bound interpretations of data. But off-radar exploration requires skepticism and imagination. Imagination can take us beyond the world we know; we need it to envision what might be. Skepticism is needed to test our speculations about the future. In business schools, we often talk about "out-of-the-box" thinking. We encourage it, but we do very little to actually develop or stimulate that capability. Imagination is about escaping gravity, escaping anything that holds us back. That's why we need to focus on creating escape velocity in the leaders for the future.

The point of this detour into corporate leadership development was to point out the need to be more predictive and anticipatory in our content. Because education is a lead sector, we need to equip the future generations who sit in our classrooms today for the future they are likely to encounter tomorrow.

Let me recap the necessary components I see that are needed in the content of formal education. First, a good grounding in a basic academic discipline is very valuable. On one hand, such grounding provides a solid foundation and an intellectual anchor for deep thought. On the other, it exposes students to scientific rigor and theoretical framing that will support and strengthen their critical thinking skills. Second, we need to become much more forward-looking, especially in applied disciplines. We cannot be backed into a cycle of perpetual just-in-time remedial efforts. Third, we need to equip students with an ability to learn (and, indeed, unlearn and relearn). With rapid change and an uncertain future, learning how to learn might well be the best skill formal education can teach future generations. It is the best (and, perhaps the only) insurance policy when faced with perpetual change.

TECHNOLOGY

Technology can (and increasingly will) enable us to fundamentally redesign and reengineer pedagogy. Such reengineering is needed if we want formal education to focus on its core responsibilities. Unfortunately, the role we have given to technology so far has been one of merely enhancing the traditional delivery model. My belief is that formal education has not even begun to explore, let alone capitalize on, technology's potential to help students develop the talent they naturally possess to its full potential.

How have we been using technology in formal education? I see three ways: 1) to animate the knowledge delivery process, 2) to create a new delivery channel, and 3) to increase geographic reach. Videos, live streaming, interactive graphics, etc. are all technology-based ways to animate and put new life into the basically passive character of the traditional delivery model. In a world where we all like to be entertained, there should be no surprise that technology has been used to bring some entertainment into education. The second use of technology has been as the backbone to online education. Traditional educational institutions, as well as newcomers in this space, use online platforms as new channels for knowledge delivery. A third use of technology has been to increase the geographic reach of the delivery. Any educational institution can now use technology to beam its delivery into every corner of the world.

With this unlimited geographic reach, schools have begun to realize that online education is also a good student recruitment tool. The challenge for many top universities, for example, is to find unusually gifted students. Universities such as MIT, Harvard, Stanford, etc. want to identify potential Nobel laureate material as that is the level they compete at with one another. With online MOOCs widely available, motivated students seek them out, and through performance assessment, schools can quickly identify where that material might be hidden. In fact, I see no reason why universities should not put a big chunk of the undergraduate (UG) curriculum online for free and then select the best-performing students to finish their degree on campus. This way, universities could focus their contact teaching on areas where that contact adds value to the students' learning. This could even be engineered as a financial win/win and might well be one trend emerging from the covid-19 lockdown experience.

Note that the current uses of technology enhance knowledge delivery in order to make it more attractive to and/or convenient for students. None really address the model itself and its focus on delivery as opposed to learning. If we want formal education to refocus on its core responsibilities as described above, we will need to go well beyond the current deployment of technology. Technology already has (and increasingly will have) capabilities that can help the development of inherent talent in affordable ways. For this to occur, the focus will need to shift from delivery to learning and from a teacher-centric world to a student-centric world. Because of technology's assessment capabilities, it will lead to more accountability as well. To stimulate some thoughts in that direction, let us explore what technology has been able to do in other sectors.

What is current technology actually capable of? Let me briefly comment on five capabilities that have already fundamentally changed other industries. There is no reason to believe that they cannot disrupt education in similar ways. My view is that they will, and we might as well stare them in the eyes and get to work. Let me also point out that a defining characteristic of current technology is that all these capabilities can be scaled and leveraged in real time. We need to fundamentally change our mindset to be able to appreciate these capabilities and integrate them into novel pedagogical models.

The five capabilities I want to focus on are: empowerment, unbundling, adaptation, intelligence, and business-model innovation.

1. **Empowerment.** Ultimately, technology empowers the user. It enables all of us to do things the way we like or enjoy doing them. By integrating more technology on the demand side (as opposed to the supply side), we could give students much more control over their learning journey. They do not have much control now as learning journeys are preprogrammed with few options to choose from. And all are executed in a teacher-centric mode as opposed to a student-centric mode. Student empowerment would require a shift from delivery to learning.

2. **Unbundling.** One of the big impacts of digital technology has been its ability to unbundle systems and processes to reveal their underlying parts. In the process, such unbundling exposes parts whose value-add might be minimal or no longer exists—the disintermediation that has come along with unbundling. As discussed above, formal education bundles knowledge into degrees. Technology could empower students to design their own learning paths in line with their potential and the deployment opportunities that potential provides. And as we have seen in other industries, disintermediation leads to restructuring as any intermediary with no role and/or value-add will be cut out. This raises an interesting question about the future role, if any, of teachers (faculty) when the attention shifts from delivery to learning. I will address that question later in the book.

3. **Adaptation.** As technology enables the scaling of microcustomization, we can easily move away from the one-size-fits-all model. In education, such adaptation would enable us to move away from the industrial-factory model with its standardized delivery across students. With an eye on the core responsibilities of formal education, the focus should shift to individual learning.

4. **Intelligence.** Technology is becoming increasingly intelligent with the ability to remember, learn, and anticipate. Building an educational system that is intelligent would enhance adaptation in real time, further enhancing efficient and effective learning. It would also avoid the remedial development cycles we see now, since anticipatory analyses would secure the alignment of talent development with future needs. As I will discuss later, lifelong learning will need an intelligent educational system as a backbone.

5. **Business-Model Innovation.** Technology has enabled companies across industries to rethink business models and diversify their sources of revenues. As discussed above, the current model of education is expensive, and in my view, not sustainable. We need to deploy technology in innovative ways to make education much more accessible and affordable.

Many businesses have relied on these capabilities to create platform models to reinvent themselves. Formal education is not a business in the traditional sense, but it is a platform at its core. It brings knowledge and students together. In fact, since many educational institutions do not own or create the knowledge they convey, they are essentially two-sided markets with knowledge input on one side and student demand on the other side. They are the physical equivalent of online platforms, such as eBay. Given this, let us look at formal education through the lens of a typical platform business and contrast its characteristics with those that make platform businesses successful. This might give us inspiration on how to rethink and redesign formal education using technology.

The success of a typical platform business depends on three design characteristics: gravity, flow, and access. Gravity refers to how effective the platform is in attracting users. For example, in the case of eBay, how effective is it in growing both the buyer space and the seller space? Both feed off one another because more buyers bring in more sellers and vice versa. Note that gravity is how platform businesses build marketing into their platforms. It is gravity that defines the success and the power of a platform in the marketplace.

The second characteristic of successful platform businesses is flow, which refers to the effective matching of the two sides in a two-sided marketplace. In the case of eBay, flow refers to how well it matches the seller of an item with potential buyers of that item. A third characteristic of successful platform businesses is access, or the ease with which both sides can engage with the platform.

Before benchmarking formal education as a physical platform against these platform design characteristics, note that platform businesses are not exclusively confined to virtual space. Some platforms, such as eBay, are pure online platforms. But many others integrate online and offline capabilities into a seamless service entity spanning both physical and virtual space. A ride-sharing service such as Uber has woven online and offline features into one magic carpet that can take any of us anywhere, anytime we want to go. Uber does not see online and offline as parallel universes. In fact, it never really uses that terminology when describing its identity and/or service.

Uber is not a bad reference point for what formal education as a platform business could be like. I am not suggesting just mapping one into the other. In fact, those of us in education can and should do better than Uber. To stretch our thinking, consider the following questions: what makes Harvard University (you can fill in the name of your own alma mater) different from Uber? Could Harvard University be Uber-like? What would that imply and look like? Should Harvard University be Uber-like?

Let us look at a typical university and benchmark its gravity, flow, and access against those of a successful platform such as, for example, Uber. As I already mentioned, any university is a two-sided market for knowledge dissemination. It links knowledge with students who need that knowledge. If it is a research university, it might have some proprietary knowledge, but beyond that, all universities have access to the same knowledge. Their libraries, for example, carry exactly the same journals and books.

A university bundles knowledge into degrees and then matches those to qualifying students who desire to pursue those degrees. Student access is not open but limited to those who measure up to the qualification standards set by the university. Different universities set different admission standards and, as a result, differ in the student profile they match with their knowledge bundles. The knowledge bundles themselves are largely undifferentiated across universities because of accreditation and certification requirements. The knowledge bundles are matched with groups of students (cohort classes) in a mechanical (bureaucratic) process where all go through the bundle at the same pace. The knowledge is conveyed by frontline faculty who have some freedom in how they slice, dice, and spice the knowledge meal they cook up and serve in their classes. In the end, the university helps with student placement. Upon graduation, students join the alumni network that will provide scaffolding support to their career path(s).

First, note that no university has been able (as yet) to create the global market power Uber has been able to do. In contrast to ride-sharing, the two-sided market for bundled knowledge is highly fragmented and regional. Just look at how many business schools there are around the world conferring MBA degrees. We have many knowledge platforms operating in parallel to one another around the world. Why is that? Could we see an Uber-like world in formal education? What would it take to create such a world?

Let us look at how formal education deploys and manages gravity, flow, and access, the keys to success for a platform business. For gravity, we need to look at both sides of the platform—how they draw in knowledge and how they draw in students. As all other educational institutions, a university has undifferentiated access to knowledge. If it is a research university with faculty actively creating new knowledge, it might have some proprietary knowledge. Whether that proprietary knowledge is readily shared on its delivery platform is a decision the university makes. If that proprietary knowledge has commercial value, a university might well keep it out of reach until legal ownership has been established. For the nonproprietary knowledge and for any university that does not create knowledge, the challenge is to find it and bridge the gap to the knowledge source so that what is provided is up-to-date.

Students are drawn to a university/degree combination

based on perceived value. The true value of an education is currently difficult to assess, but technology will at some point enable closed-loop assessment, which will be a real game changer.

Closed-loop assessment means that given my inherent talent and what I studied (what subjects, in what sequence, how, and with whom), I know what I will be good at; and if I want to be good at something, I know what inherent talent I need and what I should study (what subjects, in what sequence, how, and with whom). This type of assessment does not yet exist, but in my view, it is not a matter of "if" but of "when." Closed-loop assessment would enable measurement of the actual value of education. In its absence, we rely on surrogate assessments of value or what we call "perceived value." That value is likely to be influenced by the university's overall reputation, job-market prospects for the university/degree combination, the alumni network the university has, etc. Education is currently sold on credence benefits, but I believe technology will change all that in the future.

Flow refers to matching students with knowledge bundles (degrees). This is currently done in a standardized and mechanical way that is out of the students' control and is devoid of any intelligence. This is where I see technology making significant inroads. Furthermore, there are currently no variance plays where delivery is adapted to, for example, the variance represented in cohort classes. As I already pointed out, universities support diversity but do not capitalize on that in the pedagogical process as a source for learning. I can see some revolutionary innovations coming down the road in this area.

On the access characteristics, it is as if both sides of the two-sided education market operate at the opposite ends of the scale. On the knowledge side, the access is wide open and a university will bring in all the knowledge needed to be bundled into the degrees that it wants to provide. On the student side, however, the access is not open at all. Only students who meet the admission requirements get in. In contrast to knowledge access, student access is selective and limited. Once admitted, the engagement access is the traditional delivery model, which does not allow the student to take control over his/her learning agenda. Students find themselves on a conveyor belt where knowledge is dripped into them at a pace that they have no control over. Any adaptation and/or intelligence that can be built into flow would also revolutionize access.

Let us take a step back now and reflect on the following question: how attractive would Uber (or any other ride-sharing service for that matter) be if it operated like Harvard University? Both operate a platform model but provide vastly different services. To me, the difference between them is that one thinks as a platform while the other one does not. To deploy technology effectively in education, mindsets will have to fundamentally change.

There are really many great opportunities for technology in education but for these to materialize, the relationship between formal education and the technology sector will have to change as well. Today, that relationship is very much one of supplier-user; i.e., educational institutions buying technology products off the shelf.

When I was dean at MSM SKOLKOVO, I wanted to build a tech-based interactive classroom. I knew what I wanted it to look like and what I wanted it to be capable of, but I was not sure whether the available technology could deliver it, and if not, how long it would take for technology to be able to do so. When I approached tech companies, they were only interested in selling screens. They had little interest in listening to my vision or seeing how the available technology could deliver it. Some even left the impression that they thought education was doomed and that they would replace all of us soon. Perhaps they will, but for that to happen, they have a lot of learning ahead of them.

Technology is just a tool and can only be a solution to a problem if you know what the problem is. A good example is gaming companies getting into education. As I have observed over many years of working with business simulation games, gamified learning does enhance learning efficiency and effectiveness. But learning itself is fundamentally different from gaming. Gaming can be deployed in the learning process, but it cannot and should not be the objective of that process. Gaming knowledge is not learning that knowledge. But you can learn knowledge in a game that plays on curiosity and enables discovery. That requires an immersion in the factual reality surrounding that knowledge and not in the make-believe world of science fiction.

In sum, I believe that a partnership between education and the tech sector is needed where collaborative efforts enhance cross-learning on how needs on one side and capabilities on the other side evolve. Through collaboration and experimentation, the capabilities of new and emerging technologies can be deployed to redesign pedagogy along the following lines, from:

· efficient delivery to effective learning;
· a teacher-centric to student-centric focus;
· standardized delivery to adapted delivery;
· vertical to horizontal learning engagement;
· passive to active learning engagement;
· discrete, disjointed testing to continuous, unobtrusive assessment; and
· mechanical matching to intelligent matching.

The discussion so far has focused on technology as a tool that should be leveraged beyond what we do with it today.

It is important to point out that technology, especially smart technology, can be a source of knowledge as well, and we will witness intelligent collaboration between humans and AI systems. How AI systems and humans can or ought to work together deserves more attention than I give it here. Different approaches and styles will emerge, and we will need to develop a better understanding of how each can play to its strength and how they can exploit each other's capabilities in real time. To stimulate that thinking, I will discuss briefly how AI systems can stimulate human thought and imagination, and how they can help in developing intuitive intelligence.

AlphaGo, developed by Google, is an AI system that plays the popular game of Go. When in 2017 it beat Ke Jie, the number one Go player in the world at the time, avid players worried about what would happen to their beloved game. But when studying how the AI system played their passionate game, they discovered there was much to be learned. As in chess, opening moves are a key part of playing Go. When expert players looked at the opening moves AlphaGo made, they discovered some that they were neither familiar with, had thought about, nor had dared to play. Hence, AlphaGo opened a window on novel opening strategies, and initial dismay gave way to a newfound inspiration for the game. The jury is still out on whether this would give humans the upper hand again, but there is no denying that transparent AI systems can stimulate and even excite human thought.

AI systems can also be valuable tools in developing intuitive intelligence. As I described earlier, such intelligence will be crucial in the AI-empowered world of ambient intelligence. In his book *Gut Feelings: The Intelligence of the Unconscious*, Gerd Gigerenzer describes an example of decision-making in the intensive care unit of a Michigan hospital. As doctors' decisions were far from optimal, an AI system was developed to aid the doctors. The implementation of the system was fascinating. Behavior improved dramatically, but doctors did not continue to use the system. In initially working with the system, the doctors learned what was important and what was not. Based on that information, they developed simple heuristics that led to decisions that were nearly as good as those that the AI system recommended. The outcome was that the AI system inspired simple and transparent heuristics that led to near-optimal decision-making behavior.

For an AI system to inspire human thought and stimulate intuitive intelligence, it has to be transparent. Unfortunately, most AI systems developed today lack such transparency (which is probably another reason why many fear them). It is clearly beyond the scope of this book, but some thought ought to go into the design of new AI systems and approaches that would make them transparent. Apart from the value such transparency would bring, it would make the systems more approachable and acceptable. In sum, collaborative engagement between AI systems and humans is not an endgame but probably the beginning of a whole new adventure.

The focus of formal education has to shift back to the student and his/her learning. As I outlined earlier in the book, the responsibilities of formal education are to identify the natural gift each child has and then to provide that child with an opportunity to develop that gift to its full potential in an affordable way. With the help of technology, we need to create intelligent and collaborative co-learning ecosystems that leverage the variance in that ecosystem to the benefit of the child's learning and that recognize and build on each child's unique profile in terms of an endowed gift and cognitive learning profile. Technology can help get us out of the delivery corner that we've backed ourselves into. We need to move away from the focus on efficient delivery to a focus on effective learning. In my view, technology is the bridge to accomplish this. Its core contribution will be in learning assessment, a weak spot in formal education today. Continuous, unobtrusive assessment will create a growing knowledge base that will ultimately lead to a model of formal education that is intelligent, that is focused on learning, and that secures accountability.

CHAPTER FIVE

The Road Ahead

Lifelong Learning

The reality that is unfolding in front of us is one where we will most likely have to work longer. Retirement ages are on the rise in most developed countries because of the continued increases in life expectancy coupled with aging populations. At the same time, accelerated innovation and advancement in many fields is making knowledge obsolete at an ever-increasing pace. As a consequence, what we learn in school might make us obsolete at much younger ages unless we stay abreast of current advances. This emerging reality necessitates lifelong learning, not as a hobby or retirement fancy but as a necessary backbone to an extended professional life.

Formal education as a foundation on which to build a

career (or careers) will no longer be enough. Continued learning is needed as necessary scaffolding to enable and support the many careers future generations are likely to string together over their lifetimes. A solid foundation will remain necessary, but we will need to continue to build on that foundation in an intelligent and effective way. Lifelong learning as an integral part of anyone's life journey is on the horizon. If truly taken to heart, it offers formal education an opportunity to reinvent itself and lay the foundation for its sustainability.

To set the stage, let me first contrast lifelong learning with continuing education. Continuing education is about piling on more degrees. For example, when we go back to university to get a master's degree, we continue our formal education. In the all-then-nothing model, this is about pouring more concrete to solidify the base on which to build a professional career. Once we graduate from school, the focus distinctly shifts from learning to career development. Lifelong learning is different.

Lifelong learning is not about piling on more degrees but about fundamentally changing the path of and approach to learning. Lifelong learning should be thought of as a continuous process of building and enhancing capabilities that enable versatile deployment of those capabilities and where those deployments themselves become an integral part of a continuing learning process. Today, we talk about building a career on top of the formal education we received early in life. Tomorrow, we will talk about co-learning ecosystems that are built on top of a solid foundation and that will enable us to extend our careers and capitalize on the many career opportunities the dynamic future holds. To give some perspective on what lifelong learning might require and how we should start thinking about it, let me go back to the development of a tennis prodigy. I believe that analogy can help us understand the important ingredients needed for a true lifelong learning paradigm.

The natural talent of a tennis prodigy is mined prodigiously with the help of a co-learning ecosystem consisting of coaches, doctors, physiotherapists, dieticians, etc. The tennis prodigy relies on a team of professionals with complementary skills who individually and collectively dedicate themselves to developing the prodigy and his/her talent to its full potential. In this manner, we have a front line of many with a target of one, exactly the opposite of what we find in formal education. As discussed above, the whole approach is prodigy-centric (student-centric): identifying, scoping, developing, enhancing, and leveraging the richness of the prodigy's natural talent (or gift). The mindset of the prodigy is fully dedicated to that as well. Even when tennis stars retire from the competitive tennis circuit, they still feel there is room to learn and give to the game. In their mind, learning is not an endgame but a lifelong dedication to the pursuit of perfection.

What does that front line of professionals do exactly? Their collective focus is on developing an all-around solid tennis player with a potent weapon, i.e., a versatile player (and not a one-trick pony) with a deadly point of differentiation (which could be a serve, a backhand, a drop shot, speed, etc.). Accordingly, a solid all-around player is necessary but not sufficient. There has to be something special that can be deployed and leveraged successfully, now and into the future. That something special is what eventually will define the player on the tour, but it finds its origin in the natural talent the prodigy has. The frontline team of professionals tunes in to that something special and weaponizes it for the competitive game of tennis.

To achieve this, the frontline team works on a portfolio of competencies that are developed in parallel but not necessarily at the same pace: technical skills, tactical skills, mental strength, and physical strength. It is not about incremental piling on but cycling through the portfolio consistently and persistently. That cycling process is one of learning, unlearning, and relearning with an unrelenting persistence to improve and grow the prodigy into a competitive player with no equal.

The process of learning, unlearning, and relearning is guided by a long-term development plan that stretches out over the entire career of the tennis player. The development is paced so that the prodigy will be able to play at a high level of performance for a long period of time. Hence, the visible career (the tournaments the prodigy plays in and what the public gets to see and enjoy) is carefully but strategically managed. It is not about a quick return or peaking early and shooting all the ammo in one tournament. The entire visible career of tournament play is crafted around the potential the prodigy has and the time and effort it takes for that talent to be developed to sustainable perfection. In fact, the visible career is not just built on top of a tennis development program, but it is an integral part of that program. It is also not about being at it all the time. The development program contains breaks for important time away from the grind. Unfortunately, many players are forced to take breaks because of an injury. But even beyond those, pit stops are made to get body, mind, and soul back together. To extend a career at top level, nothing can be ignored and nothing can be left behind.

Science-based intelligence drives the talent development program. Data is collected and analyzed continuously to assess, adjust, and reassess the development plan and approach. The program evolves but without any team member ever taking his or her eyes off the ball. Adjustments are made to the evolution of the game, the evolution of technology in the game, and the competence profile of likely opponents. Nothing is fixed or cast in stone except for the unwavering focus on the prodigy and his or her talent. The prodigy is the point of gravity in a co-learning ecosystem. None of this is age-dependent. It is all talent-dependent. It is the richness of the prodigy's talent and his/her character and personality that drive the entire development program.

A key person in the co-learning ecosystem is the coach. A unique partnership develops between him or her and the prodigy. Jointly, they weave together on-circuit and off-circuit play into a career-long process of learning and development that fits the prodigy's profile and his/her capabilities. In that process, the coach plays multiple roles. These roles include teaching the technical and tactical aspects of playing tennis at a competitive level but go well beyond that. They involve shaping the prodigy not only as a superb athlete but also as a maturing person with the understanding that one cannot be separated from the other. In fact, good coaches look at how one can solidify the other. Accordingly, they take a holistic view and pursue the development of the complete package: a better athlete and a better person. Ethics are intertwined with the love of competing and persistent striving for improvement. To them, the development of body, mind, and soul is as important as the development of muscles. The coach is a constant shadow over all aspects of the maturing athlete's life as his/her natural talent is weaponized.

Let me reflect on this analogy. Earlier in the book, I contrasted the approach with how we develop human intelligence in formal education: the focus on teaching as opposed to learning, the teacher-centric approach as opposed to the student-centric approach, and the standardization of the industrial-factory model characterizing formal education as opposed to the complete adaptation of talent development to the prodigy's profile and the nature of his/her talent. With the analogy as a backdrop, let's look at how we should think about lifelong learning. In that regard, formal education as we know it cannot give much guidance as it has largely outsourced the learning part and has evolved into an efficient knowledge-delivery service. Furthermore, lifelong learning is too critical to our future to just stretch a deficient model for a quick fix. I believe that an entirely new paradigm is needed and that the tennis analogy can guide us in shaping that paradigm.

What should the objective of lifelong learning be? We all have a gift rich in potential if we take the time to fully discover it. The objective of lifelong learning should be to devise an adaptive and intelligent co-learning ecosystem that secures continuous enhancement and versatile deployment of that potential throughout one's life. The key is talent development and not career development. The latter should be seen as just an ingredient in the process of honing the former. Similar to on-circuit tournament play for a tennis prodigy, career deployments are practical lessons in the shaping and weaponizing of one's talent.

Focusing on continuous talent development and enhancement opens up a funnel of career opportunities. In contrast, focusing on career development traps one into the cone of an ever-narrowing career path. Rafael (Rafa) Nadal, the King of Clay, would have never won the 20 Grand Slam singles titles he won (so far) if his objective was to be the King of Clay. It is doubtful he would have won the French Open a record 13 times (so far) if he was not the all-around player he truly is.

What does the honing of talent and the persistent striving for improvement of that talent require? Honing talent takes time and is never fully completed, because there is always room for improvement. It is a never-ending process, a journey with no end in sight. No one will ever graduate from lifelong learning. As it is a long journey, one should start early, mentally prepare for it, commit to it, build support, plan ahead, and enjoy the ride. As such, I would argue that we need to develop a paradigm for lifelong learning first and then work back from there to redesign formal education to fit that paradigm (and not the other way around). Before exploring that, let me highlight three requirements that I see emerging from the tennis analogy for lifelong learning to be successful: mindset, support, and planning. Let's look at these three components of success and see how they could shape a lifelong learning paradigm.

MINDSET

A true learning mindset will be the engine that drives life-long learning. Besides that learning mindset, it will also be important to acquire a drive to execute. Learning and continuously striving for improvement is a grind. It takes hard work and requires sacrifice. Developing one's natural talent requires mental strength and stamina. As I wrote earlier, parents have the responsibility to instill a learning mindset in their children. For lifelong learning to work, parents also need to shape the character of their children so they understand that the only way around work is hard work. Mental preparedness and a readiness to commit will ease the pain of the continued learning grind.

We will also have to change our views on learning. Too many of us associate learning with going to school, which in turn brings up negative images and thoughts. Just look at how much joy we have at graduation: we made it! Well, there will be no graduation from lifelong learning. Learning will become a never-ending journey, and that will require a more positive view of learning and the learning process. It can no longer be something we feel we have to do but something we really want to do. We will have to learn to enjoy learning and find satisfaction in the progress we make along our journey of lifelong learning.

SUPPORT

Lifelong learning is not a journey for the lone traveler. The African proverb we all know is very apt here: "If you want to travel fast, go alone; if you want to travel far, go together." No tennis prodigy (or any sport's prodigy for that matter) ever made it entirely on their own. There was always a team of dedicated professionals and friends to guide, support, teach, comfort, and share in the grind. Lifelong learning is about traveling far, not traveling fast. It is about delving deep into the richness of one's natural talent while developing and enhancing it to secure persistent access to career opportunities as these unfold in the changing environment. Because of this, I believe that true lifelong learning requires a co-learning ecosystem to scaffold the continued enhancement and deployment of talent. As with the tennis prodigy, a group of professionals individually and collectively support the individual in his/her learning journey and together discover and learn the best path forward to succeed in that journey; i.e., what to learn when, how to learn it, what is required to learn it, how the learning can be weaponized, and in what context it can be deployed and how. Depending on the nature of the talent and the deployment opportunities for that talent, who forms part of the ecosystem will vary and could change over time. But all members are dedicated to the parallel development of the individual and his/her talent into a maturing entity with boundless deployment opportunities.

It is inspiring to look at how many of us use alumni networks to scaffold our career development and enhancement. Those networks are ecosystems that evolve. Lifelong learning needs a similar kind of support ecosystem but one that is dedicated to learning.

PLANNING

When we go on a long trip, we prepare and plan. We don't just jump in the car and drive off. We pack what we might need and map out the stages of the trip as best we can. We also don't drive or fly all the time. We build in stops to sit back and relax and take in the scenery. We also build in some slack as we are not entirely sure what we might come across and might want to take advantage of. Most of us don't like packing, but we almost all have a smile on our face when we finally pull out of the driveway. We are on our way and ready to enjoy whatever is ahead.

Lifelong learning is a journey, a long journey that requires a development plan that maps out and guides continued learning and talent enhancement for versatile deployment. That plan should consist of two interconnected components. Similar to constructing a new building, we first lay a foundation and then erect scaffolding on and around that foundation to be able to build on top of it. The higher we want to build, the deeper and the stronger the foundation will need to be. In other words, the foundation has to be solid enough for us to build on it. Building that solid foundation is the first component of the lifelong learning plan.

If we step back for a minute and consider formal education as a possible foundation for lifelong learning, we realize that the foundation is built without much thought of how it could help or reinforce continued learning and talent enhancement. At best, that foundation is built as an entry point into a professional career. It is not built with lifelong learning in mind. In fact, in formal education, lifelong learning seems to be an afterthought. It clearly should not be if formal education wants to be part of lifelong learning. Formal education should pour concrete with the objective of the foundation supporting continued learning.

To achieve that, I believe the foundation should cover two areas: the identification and development of the natural talent we all have, and the acquisition of skills and competencies needed for lifelong learning. In the case of intellectual talent, a solid grounding in a traditional academic discipline would serve us well. Such grounding would not only provide the student with disciplinary knowledge but would also introduce him/her to the two cornerstones of critical thinking: scientific rigor and theoretical framing.

The foundation should also expose students to skills and competencies that would make lifelong learning easier. First, becoming truly info literate would enable students to intelligently tap into the vast amounts of information we have access to these days. As pointed out already, exposure to scientific rigor through grounding in a traditional academic discipline would facilitate such literacy. Second, students should be exposed to and acquire learning skills and techniques. Just take a step back and reflect on this: we all go to school to learn, but we are never really taught how to learn! We are left to our own wits to discover how we could best learn and, regrettably, some of us never do. For lifelong learning to be effective, we need to be taught how to learn, unlearn, and relearn given our cognitive learning profile and the nature and character of our inherent talent.

With a solid foundation in place, a plan for how to build on top of that foundation over time will need to be developed. This plan should not only cover continued enhancement of the talent but should also cover the development of the individual. Hence, the focus should be on the complete package: talent and person. On the talent side, the plan should map out how to update, enhance, fine-tune, and weaponize talent for versatile deployment. Versatility is key here as sustained disruption will shorten certain careers but will also give rise to new career opportunities. Accordingly, I believe the focus in lifelong learning should not be on career development but on the continued enhancement of talent that would secure access to any career opportunity sustained disruption might bring along.

As talent is embodied in a person, that person will need to be brought along as well. Accordingly, successful talent deployment will require nurturing of the love for competing, a continued striving for perfection, and the acquisition of a sound and solid moral compass. In sum, as the talent matures, so does the person with that talent.

Looking back at the tennis analogy, I believe that a development plan for lifelong learning should have the following five characteristics:

- **Co-developed.** Lifelong learning is ultimately about self-development and self-enhancement, but how to approach that and how to do that requires input, help, and support from professionals with different perspectives and competencies. The plan should be drawn up with input from all members of the co-learning ecosystem and it should become a working document that guides lifelong learning.
- **Adaptive.** The long-term development plan should be fully adapted in content, pace, and timing to the cognitive learning profile of the individual, the nature and character of that individual's talent and its potential, and the character of that individual. It should also be sensitive to context and time.
- **Paced.** The long-term development plan should not follow the clockwise, regimented pace of formal education. At times, the pace could be accelerated. At other

times, it will need to slow down or even stop. Taking a break to step back, think, and reflect is important to secure learning. Furthermore, mind, body, and soul all need to be brought along in lifelong learning. As all three do not necessarily develop and mature at the same pace, pit stops will be needed to realign them so nothing gets left behind.

- **Intelligent.** The long-term development plan has to be forward-looking and not backward-correcting. It should have memory, be able to learn, and anticipate the next step(s).
- **Science-based.** Continued cycles of assessment, adjustment, and reassessment will be required in lifelong learning. Like the case of the tennis prodigy, scientific assessment should drive learning, unlearning, and relearning so that the talent enhancement stays on track.

In summary, the success of lifelong learning will depend on mindset, support, and planning. Collectively, all three elements shape a new lifelong learning paradigm. The question posed now is what the role of formal education could or should be in this paradigm. What can or should it contribute? Before considering this question, let me share with you the link between lifelong learning and the natural curiosity we are all born with.

As humans, we are born discoverers. We are curious, eager

to explore, and ready to learn. Recall the story of my daughter encountering a blacksmith for the first time. The novelty of the situation and the passion she sensed as the blacksmith hammered away ignited wonder and an eagerness in her to know more. Young children naturally and playfully explore the world around them to learn about it. When they enter formal education (increasingly at younger ages), they find themselves in a structured learning environment where they are told what to learn (but not how). In fact, we are all born learners, but formal schooling makes us students. There is more than a subtle difference between being a learner and being a student.

A learner seeks knowledge, but a student is taught to seek success. Even at very early ages, school teaches children to collect stars, smiley faces, or whatever the incentive is that the teacher uses to mold compliant learning behavior. Gone is the freely wondering curiosity we are born with! That natural inclination has to make room for an artificial process where *painful application* (which is the Latin origin of the word "student") is the way to acquire knowledge. As formal learning is somewhat akin to solitary confinement (homework in solitude), it is almost as if play has to make room for pain!

What happens then to our natural curiosity and ease with which we learn when we are pulled into formal education's sphere of gravity? Does compliant behavior blunt natural curiosity? Does it get suppressed or subverted? Do we lose our natural urge to discover and learn? These are worthwhile questions to ponder because (a) lifelong learning is not synonymous with being a lifelong student (i.e., piling on degrees), and (b) we seem to bring formal education to younger and younger ages (even pre-kindergarten is looking more and more like formal schooling today). Let me share a story with you about three-year-old Evan. This story always comes to my mind when I reflect on what might happen to each and every one of us when we as children enter the clutches of formal education.

The context is an experiment run by the *Washington Post* in 2007 (and later repeated). Joshua Bell, a world-renowned concert violinist, was asked to play in the L'Enfant Plaza Metro Station in Washington, DC (as an interesting side note, as you read on, keep in mind that "l'enfant" means "the child" in French). Just inside the door of the subway station, he played his prized Stradivarius for about 45 minutes. As a street musician, he had put his violin case out to collect money from passersby. The objective of the experiment was to observe what people passing by in the busy metro station would do.

The video of the experiment is available on YouTube. The main statistics of what happened are as follows: 1,017 people passed by, 27 dropped money in his violin case, and only seven people stopped and listened. Furthermore, during the 45 minutes Joshua played various violin concertos, he collected less than what one ticket would cost to see him play in concert. Perhaps that's not surprising given the busy society we have become. The interesting aspect of the experiment for us here is the profile of the seven people who did stop and listen. One was a person who recognized Joshua (and dropped a $20 note in his violin case). Another was a gentleman who leaned back against the wall and obviously enjoyed the private concert neither realizing who nor what violin he was listening to. And then there was three-year-old Evan.

Evan walked up, stopped, and listened until his mom pulled him away to move on. Evan was not the only child who did this during the 45-minute experiment. We have no idea what drew Evan's attention and curiosity, but something did. Was it the music? Was it the sound of the $2.5 million Stradivarius? Was it the quality of play? Was it the passion and competence Joshua brought to his play? We will never know. What we do know is that Evan had no idea who Joshua Bell was, what unique and prized instrument he was playing, or what classical pieces he was playing. Evan's reaction was pure and natural. His reaction was not learned behavior. In fact, I am pretty sure that among the many people who did walk past Joshua in those 45 minutes were students of classical music and/or the violin. Accordingly, those who got formal training and should know and recognize the beauty of Joshua's play moved on while unspoiled

Evan did not. That is until his mom tugged him away. The students ignored him while the natural learner noticed and listened!

What did the tugging away do to Evan's natural curiosity? Let's keep in mind that what Evan's mom did is pretty much what all parents would have done in the same situation. As formal education does not seem to build on, strengthen, or leverage that natural curiosity, it just lays a set of new and more formal learning tracks on top of it. Does that have consequences similar to the tugging away? Do these actions blunt in any way the natural and unspoiled curiosity we are born with? It would be a shame if they did because that curiosity is the seed from which a learning mindset could develop. It is exactly that mindset that will drive lifelong learning. Perhaps, as educators and as parents (who are responsible for nurturing a learning mindset in our children), we should rethink what we do and give nature a chance. After all, we would all benefit in our lifelong learning journey from rediscovering and leveraging the natural curiosity we are born with.

From the perspective of lifelong learning adopted here, it is evident that few, if any, educational institutions have embraced the opportunity. Perhaps it's not all that surprising given that formal education has moved away from learning to focus on efficient delivery. One can of course always go back to school for another degree, but that is not lifelong learning as it's envisioned here. Pretty much no educational institution provides any learning support for their graduates after graduation day. In fact, on that day, all plugs are pulled out except for one—the alumni plug. But that plug is not linked to learning in any significant or meaningful way. From the institutions' perspective, alumni are mostly PR subjects and donor targets. From the graduates' perspective, alumni networks provide useful scaffolding support in career development and advancement. In contrast to the educational institutions themselves, well-functioning alumni networks are quite dynamic and responsive and, almost entirely on their own, have become evolving ecosystems for career support. They very much operate like the co-learning ecosystems that I see as necessary to lifelong learning but with a narrower bandwidth and exclusive concentration on career development and enhancement (and deployment of talent). Learning is secondary, and lifelong learning is not on their radar yet.

The impetus and momentum for change might well come from engaged alumni networks as they are likely to be the first to witness the consequences of the emerging reality and as such understand the need for lifelong learning. For educational institutions, these alumni networks provide a window into that emerging reality, but unfortunately it's a window very few look through. In that regard, educational institutions might want to rethink their views on and use of alumni and alumni networks. As I will point out shortly, alumni networks might represent a lifeline into a strategic opportunity for formal education to reinvent itself. Before exploring that, what exactly are the play options for formal education when it comes to lifelong learning?

Within the lifelong learning paradigm I laid out above, formal education could adopt three roles: be a supplier, be a partner, or be the owner. Formal education could, for example, provide the foundation for lifelong learning and leave continued learning and personal development and enhancement to others. It would still require them to refocus on student-centric learning, adhere to the core responsibilities as described earlier in the book, and provide a foundation that would enable lifelong learning. Of the three roles they could play in lifelong learning, this is the one closest to what they are doing right now.

Besides just being a supplier, formal education could also opt to become a partner in the co-learning ecosystem. Could they, for example, play the role of coach? What would that require from them and imply for them? The third role formal education could play in lifelong learning would be to move into it with full commitment and try to own that space. I see this third role very much as an opportunity for formal education to reinvent itself and secure its sustainability. This option would require them to completely identify with lifelong learning and reengineer everything they do from that perspective. It would require major changes in mindset, focus, and operation, but with the emerging reality necessitating lifelong learning, it might be the only option for them to remain credible in the learning space. Fortunately for them, the emerging reality provides a convincing story for the needed changes, because business-as-usual will no longer be an option. Formal education might do well to keep in mind that it is much better to lead change and capitalize on the opportunities it provides than to ignore it and then get swamped by it. As any good surfer knows, if you want to ride a wave, you have to be ahead of it. And the wave is coming.

To give some perspective on what it might take to go for the strategic opportunity, let us look at how the relationship between an educational institution and its students would change. Fundamental changes (each with significant consequences) would occur both in the length and in the nature of that relationship. As one would never really graduate from lifelong learning, there would be no endpoint to the relationship (except, perhaps, with the retirement of the student). No graduation also implies no alumni, and the number of students in the co-learning ecosystem would grow over time, changing the scale of operation for any educational institution. In fact, all alumni would remain as students in the institution's learning sphere. The increased length of the relationship would also imply that the age range of students in the learning ecosystem would be much wider than what it is today. This might imply opportunities for variance plays that enrich and enhance the learning for everyone in the ecosystem.

Furthermore, admitting a student would entail a lifelong commitment to engage with that student in a partnership that would evolve and mature over time. It would be a co-learning partnership with both parties learning about the process of lifelong learning and how to adjust and fine-tune that process to the specificities of each student in his/her quest to fully develop and deploy his/her inherent talent. In contrast to the more vertical relationship between teacher and student we have in formal education today (with, of course, the student on the bottom), that co-learning partnership would be more horizontal with both sides on an equal footing in an enduring, collaborative learning effort.

The challenges for any educational institution to pull this off are significant. To appreciate those challenges, let us look at how their front lines would have to be reengineered. I can see immediately four areas where they would essentially have to flip exactly what they are doing now.

First is the front line size. As I already pointed out, they would have to go from a front line of one-to-many to one of many-to-one. Specifically, instead of the teacher-centric model of one teacher for many students, they would need to flip this to a student-centric model of many "teachers" for just one student. I wrote "teachers" because the front line would need to be a team of professionals (that might include traditional teachers) who would pair up with a particular student in a co-learning partnership. That frontline team of professionals would be unique and different for each student. Hence, the first flip would be an increase in the bandwidth and variance of the expertise collaborating with each student.

A second change educational institutions would need to make is to flip the support cone. In the current model, the frontline teacher sits on top of a cone with a whole administrative organization backing him/her up. They would need to flip this cone upside down so that the bottom becomes the diverse front line, which is then backed up by a small but agile support system that operates intelligently in alignment with the frontline team. This flip would require a declaration of war on the administrative structures that in many educational institutions have morphed into dead-weight bureaucracies that do not serve students in any meaningful way on their learning journey.

A third flip would be in the performance assessment of the frontline team. In that assessment, the focus should be on the student's career. As with the tennis prodigy, the performance of the coach and his/her support team is judged by how well the prodigy ends up performing on the tour and not independent from it. I know of no educational institution that currently assesses teachers/faculty on how well their students eventually do in their careers. I believe that lifelong learning will necessitate such an assessment and bring some accountability where it is needed but currently lacking.

A fourth flip would be in the bundling of knowledge. As the attention would shift from the supply side to the demand side, knowledge should be bundled around each student (recognizing the nature and richness of his/her talent) and not around standardized degrees (independent from the student). No tennis coach follows a standardized, off-the-shelf manual to develop and grow the prodigy under his/her stewardship. The approach he/she will follow is uniquely crafted around the prodigy, his/her talent, and the potential of that talent. This flip is one from standardization to adaptation.

Just considering these four flips, the challenges for any educational institution to take on the strategic opportunity to own lifelong learning appear significant. Indeed, from the perspective of the model and approach we have become accustomed to, they seem almost unachievable. But that is exactly the perspective you shouldn't take if you want to position yourself well for the future and to secure your credibility and sustainability in the learning space. Looking carefully at each of these challenges, they signal exciting avenues and opportunities for shaping a meaningful paradigm for lifelong learning. Embracing the learning that would occur in the process of exploring these avenues and opportunities would solidify the credibility of the educational institution, position it as a learning organization, and put it on a path to become a driving force in true lifelong learning.

CHAPTER SIX

Business Model and Accountability

How can we make formal education more affordable when lifelong learning will require more and not less from it? This must be a question gnawing at many of you. Formal education is already expensive, and if the prevailing business model was extended into lifelong learning, it would become prohibitively expensive. There are ways to subsidize tuition costs within the current model (and I discussed some already), but I believe we need new models and approaches. I also believe we need to hold formal education accountable so it remains anchored and does not drift away from its core responsibilities under the many pressures it faces. The current business model creates pressures that can hijack (and to some extent already have) the educational process. Some novel thinking is needed around business models that neither pose a threat to the integrity of the educational process nor prevent education from becoming more accessible and affordable.

To push in that direction, I want to provoke some out-of-the-box thinking on the subject. Some of you might not like where I am going, but that is fine. After all, anything outside of the box will have its critics. To maintain some focus, I will put forward a business model that has interested me for a while and that I tried to implement at one point. I will share with you my thoughts and reflections on it. The model has potential, but there are no doubt others. My objective is to stimulate thought. I will go out on a limb just so that you can see that the tree of creativity has many branches. As I am a firm believer in holding formal education accountable, I will explore a business model that has accountability embedded in it. It's my attempt at killing two birds with one stone.

Inspiration for how business models and accountability could be aligned can be found in pay-for-success mechanisms. These mechanisms have been applied to a number of social challenges, such as recidivism, homelessness, etc. Surprising to me, they have not as yet made their way into mainstream education. After all, I cannot think of a bigger social challenge than what we face in education today. To frame the discussion, let me describe the general structure of a pay-for-success mechanism first and explore that mechanism as a possible business model for formal education. There are plenty of challenges in implementing these mechanisms, but let those not cloud our thinking at this stage.

The starting point in a pay-for-success mechanism is a *challenge*, typically a social challenge. In the case of recidivism, the challenge is the high reincarceration rates we see in many countries. In the US, the rate is especially high, implying that once a person has been in jail, chances are high that person will end up in jail again. Solving the challenge would have a significant *impact*. In the case of recidivism, any program that could bring down the reincarceration rate would provide significant savings, because the cost of keeping an inmate in jail is significant (on average, more than $30,000/year in the US).

A service provider proposes a *solution* to the challenge but cannot guarantee its success. In other words, there is a chance that the proposed solution might not deliver. For example, a not-for-profit organization has developed a program to work with inmates to bring down their likelihood of reincarceration. As that program has an unproven record, there are no guarantees it will deliver on that promise.

An investor steps up to take on the *risk* and gives the service provider the capital needed to run the program. The beneficiary (in the case of the recidivism example, the government is the beneficiary as it would save money on the cost of operating jails) agrees to a *payout* to the investor but only if the program is successful. That payout would be less than the benefit the beneficiary would gain but more than the service provider's cost of running the program. Hence, the payout would guarantee a return on investment (ROI) for the investor. To illustrate this in simple numbers, if the savings were 100 and the cost to run the program was 60, the beneficiary might agree to a payout of, for example, 80. Accordingly, upon success and only upon success, the investor would receive the capital invested (60) plus an ROI on that investment of 20. Note that in the mechanism, the payout trigger is the *success* of the program. If the program does not achieve the predetermined impact, there would be no payout.

Accordingly, the pay-for-success mechanism has three parties: a service provider, a beneficiary, and an investor. The motivation for these three parties to go into a pay-for-success agreement is the potential gain each could achieve. The service provider would get risk-free capital to run his/her program. The beneficiary would not have to pay anything unless there is impact and it does not risk any capital. The investor would make a return on his/her investment when the program is successful. The basic mechanism is simple, but there are quite a few pieces that need to come together to make it work. Still, it merits exploration and could perhaps inspire us to consider adopting it (or some variant of it) in formal education. What I like about the mechanism is that: (a) it links a business model to accountability for social impact; (b) it could open up formal education to private capital while preserving its not-for-profit character and independence; and (c) the explicit assessment of impact, success, and risk would bring much needed transparency to formal education and, as a result, strengthen our trust in it.

How could a pay-for-success mechanism work in formal education? Of the three parties involved in the mechanism, formal education would be the service provider. We could take the core responsibilities of formal education as described above and unbundle them into well-defined challenges with impact targets that could be achieved by addressing those challenges. Educational institutions could then devise programs to tackle each of the challenges with the aim of achieving those impact targets. For example, consider the responsibility of formal education to discover the natural gift that each child has as early as possible. Devising a program that could do this would benefit not only the child but potentially society at large. Just consider society's loss if we missed out on identifying the next Einstein!

With suggested programs in place to address each challenge, an educational institution could approach private investors for the capital needed to run their programs. There is, of course, a risk that the programs might not achieve their set impact targets (which is also the case for any educational program in place today). After all, no educational institution would guarantee the success of their programs. Investors would assess the risk and might be willing to take it on if the return-on-investment is commensurate to that risk (higher returns for higher risk). Upon successful completion, and only then, a beneficiary would pay the investor the amount of the original investment in the programs plus a return.

The key question in fitting formal education into a pay-for-success mechanism is: who would benefit from the impact of the programs and be willing to disburse a payment when they turn out to be successful? In the example given above about talent assessment, I put forward that society would benefit greatly from identifying (and nurturing) Einstein-like intellect. But who is "society"? We would need to be very specific on who and in what way they would benefit.

In traditional pay-for-success applications, the beneficiary is a party who would gain in financial terms. It could, for example, be the government because of budget savings as in the case of the recidivism example. In the twilight of my academic career, I toyed with the idea of creating a new business school in the Gulf that would focus on identifying and developing entrepreneurial talent. Its aim would have been to create a small number of successful startups each year that would benefit the region and would draw in talent that the region currently lacked. Practicing what the school would preach, I explored the school being financed through a pay-for-success mechanism with local government entities and sovereign wealth funds as investor targets. We built an extensive model of how a limited number of successful startups would benefit the local economy in terms of incremental employment, increased tax revenues, etc. In the end, we assessed how much the creation of a few startups annually would contribute to the local GDP. Depending on how we defined success (and you need to be very specific), we came up with a range of a few percentage points! That is not exactly an insignificant impact. The whole exercise was quite educational and a true eye-opener in terms of the economic impact targeted educational programs could actually achieve.

In general, defining social impact and assessing it in monetary terms can be a challenge. As social impact of formal education is both broad and deep, I believe that we should start mapping it out in as much detail as possible and identify who might benefit from it and in what way. Such mapping would be valuable beyond pay-for-success mechanisms as it would clearly lay out the impact education can have and solidify its credibility.

Do the benefits necessarily have to be monetary ones? The question is worth asking because there could be situations where the benefits of social impact are nonmonetary or they are difficult to assess in monetary terms. Consider, for example, the philanthropic activities that private companies often engage in as part of their corporate social responsibilities (CSR). When a company decides to bankroll a program to help, for example, the elderly in a community to receive prepared meals at home, it would not directly benefit from that financially. What it might gain from supporting such a program is visibility and a positive image in that community. That public relations (PR) benefit could be quite important and valuable to that company even if its exact value is difficult to assess monetarily. If such nonmonetary benefits could be integrated in pay-for-success mechanisms, the pool of beneficiaries (and, as a result, the applicability of the mechanisms) would expand.

Let me explore the PR example a bit further as it might hold some promise for formal education. Perhaps, as part of their corporate social responsibilities, private companies might be interested in underwriting educational projects that are risky but would have a significant social impact when successfully executed. Recall that in a pay-for-success mechanism, the beneficiary's payout is contingent on success. Unless the pre-defined impact is achieved, the beneficiary would not have to pay anything. Accordingly, a pay-for-success mechanism would secure that every PR penny goes to a winner. Then, the private company would not have to pay anything for the local community program to help the elderly unless that program was successful in achieving its objective (two hot meals a day to 1,000 elderly people within one month). It would have to pay a premium to obtain that guarantee, but it would not take on any risk. Many CSR projects do contain risks, and corporate image is a valuable commodity that can be easily and quickly tarnished. Accordingly, it is not inconceivable to think of CSR as an area where pay-for-success could find some fertile ground. If companies are looking for impactful social projects with substantial visibility, education ought to be high on the list. I could easily see expanding the pool of beneficiaries of the social impact of education to include private companies that engage in CSR activities. We would, however, need to devise a model to calculate the risk premiums these companies would need to pay to secure risk-free PR. But that is a challenge that in my view is not insurmountable.

So far, I have described the pay-for-success mechanism as having a single investor and a single beneficiary. Could we have more than one of each in a single project? In principle, the pay-for-success mechanism can handle multiple investors and multiple beneficiaries. Each investor could contribute part of the capital needed to run the program and share the ROI proportionally to his/her contribution. Each beneficiary would contribute to the payout in a prearranged way (proportional to the benefit each gains). It might be somewhat complex to execute, and perhaps it could create the need to engage intermediaries to structure such deals. But the benefit of being able to pool investors and/or beneficiaries would be that projects that have larger capital needs could also be folded into pay-for-success mechanisms.

The key to making a pay-for-success mechanism work in general is the definition and assessment of success. What impact will be pursued and how, when, and by whom will that impact be assessed? Consider for a minute what the impact might be of not getting serious about lifelong learning given the emerging reality. If we live longer and are expected to work longer but face being outdated sooner, we might become unemployable at younger ages and earlier in our professional careers. What could be some of the consequences of that? One might be that we need to rely on unemployment benefits sooner and for a longer period of time. This could put a strain on the family's finances, which itself could trigger a host of other consequences, such as mortgage defaults, broken families, children not having access to proper education, etc. It could also give rise to mental health issues and/or substance abuse as a result of the loss of self-esteem. A whole cascade of negative effects could be triggered. Any program addressing lifelong learning would have to look at these (and many others) and decide on what social impact would be targeted with the program, how that impact would be measured and when, and who would be tasked with that measurement.

With the current appetite for and interest in data analytics, I do not see any major obstacle to start building social-impact maps and assessment databases for all the core responsibilities of formal education. Apart from enabling pay-for-success mechanisms that would inherently hold formal education accountable, this exercise would also provide a much better and deeper understanding of the true value formal education provides. That might help in restoring an appreciation for and trust in formal education. The question I leave you to reflect on is whether formal education would want to be held accountable in such a specific and measurable way.

CHAPTER SEVEN

Where Do We Go from Here?

We are all born rough diamonds waiting to be discovered, waiting to be studied for the unique potential we hold, waiting to be cut to reveal the natural sparkle we inherently have. Formal education has the responsibility to identify that potential, develop it, and provide a path for its continued enhancement. We all deserve the cut that will truly reveal what nature has endowed us with and that will secure its continued brilliance for all to enjoy. As my random walk of observations and reflections reveals, some fundamental changes in formal education are in order to secure a perfect and affordable cut for all.

The future of formal education is about enabling and supporting lifelong learning. Such learning will secure sustained enhancement and versatile deployment of our unique talent, and it will nurture our growth as human beings. As my thoughts in the book reveal, getting there will require changes in pedagogy, in the educational process, in the business model, in the mindset, and in the focus of formal education. Those changes will shape a much-needed new paradigm for true lifelong learning. The reality that is unfolding around us necessitates such a paradigm but has also provided us with a pivotal moment to get to work on it.

The COVID-19 pandemic and its aftermath have created a crisis in education (and beyond). As crises often do, they hold opportunities to think and work on much-needed change. In education, we should not waste any time straightening the dominos where they fell. We need to pick them all up and put them where we want them to fall. That requires careful thought about the pattern we should lay them out in. A strategic opportunity lies in having true lifelong learning shape that pattern and provide us with a much-needed new paradigm for education.

The observations and reflections I shared in this book are meant to inspire initial thoughts about what that new paradigm might look like. I pulled at a few strands but not all. Some of the ones I did pull probably need a stronger tug. Much more thought and reflection is needed. This book pulls open the accordion of formal education to suck in fresh air, but more air is needed before we can play a tune, any tune. Pulling the accordion farther open will broaden our perspective and deepen our understanding of what formal education has become, could be, and should be. I need you to pull with me so that we eventually can play the education tune future generations need and deserve.

No doubt you have thoughts of your own, some triggered by those I shared in the book. Reflect on your own thoughts, write them down, and share them with the online Rough Diamonds community of concerned readers and committed change agents. Some of my own reflections continue to ramify in all sorts of intellectually intoxicating directions, and I will share those as well to stimulate further thought and amplify the momentum for change.

I believe that collective reflection and engagement will shape a mindset that can and will deliver what we owe future generations. It will also fuel our imagination on what could be. Exciting new and creative ideas will undoubtedly emerge. We owe it to future generations to explore them all.

Given the uncertain reality many of you in education face, you might feel pinned against the wall with your minds anchored in the now and a tendency to grasp at what could be saved from the past. You need to free your minds and think about the future generations in your care. Their future and not your past should occupy you now.

We all have a lot of learning to do, and we have the responsibility to do it now. Learning is our lifeline now; continued learning will be that of future generations.

Acknowledgments

Thoughts and reflections are shaped by observations one makes, by people one meets and engages with, and by experiences one has over time. Mine keep me intellectually engaged and curious. They also fascinate me for the many new paths they offer for further thought, discovery, learning, and growth.

For all this, I am immensely grateful to many people I met on my path: students, teachers and mentors, colleagues, friends and family. I owe a lot to the many students I have had over the years and across the world. Many of you taught me a lot more than I ever taught you! I am also grateful to my own teachers and mentors who inspired me, motivated me, and set me on the path I took. Thanks are also due to my friends, my family, and many wonderful colleagues I had the privilege of working with. I didn't always agree with you or like what you told me, but your frankness broadened my perspective on many issues. Without all of you, I would not be who I am and would not have acquired the richness of experience and the depth of perspective that enabled me to write this book. Every thought and reflection in this book is mine, but your thumbprints are all over it. To all of you, a heartfelt thank-you.

Many gave me opportunities to makes mistakes. This book is dedicated to you. Because of you, I did live a dream. A lot of what I learned is captured in the thoughts and reflections conveyed in this book. Without you, I would not have acquired these lessons and never would have been able to write this book. You got to know me well, and I doubt that any of you will be surprised about anything I share in the book. I was always quite transparent and readily shared what was on my mind. It didn't always come out the way it should, but you always knew exactly where I stood. That is what I aim to achieve with this book as well. Your gift to me did benefit me immensely, but I want that benefit to be shared with future generations who depend on us to prepare and equip them for their future.

Many of the reflections expressed in this book crystalized when I spent six months as a visiting research scholar at the MIT Sloan School of Management. It was one of the few academic sabbaticals I took during my career but unquestionably the most reflective and rewarding one. I owe a heartfelt thanks to my many friends at MIT Sloan. You were solid and supportive partners when we built MSM SKOLKOVO, and you gave me the academic perch that I needed in the twilight of my academic career to reflect on my experience in education across three continents. None of you are in any way responsible for what I penned down in this book, but you gave me the opportunity to reflect on my global experiences. Without you, much of my learning would have been lost.

A big thank-you to Carol, who meticulously typed and corrected the many drafts and revisions of this book. Yes, I wrote the draft with pen on paper, the old-fashioned way. I somehow never accepted computers being typewriters and, hence, never acquired word-processing skills. As I see my daughter practicing her French handwriting in the beautiful attaché script, I am happy I stuck to my bias.

Thanks are also due to all of you who volunteered to read an early draft of the book. English not being my native language, you had to struggle through some creative grammar and erroneous punctuation. Thanks for putting up with it and remaining focused on the content I was trying to convey. Your feedback made this a much better book.

The Scribe Media team harnessed my academic temperament to make sure this book saw the light of day. Thanks for your help, support, and encouragement along the way and for making sure that the end product was really my book.

Finally, a heartfelt thanks to my wife, Julia, and my princess, Angelica. They have to put up with a husband and a dad whose head is not always there. Reflections have a way of grabbing your mind and not letting loose. And mine tends to ramify in all sorts of intellectually intoxicating directions. Thanks for always being there for me.

About the Author

DR. WILFRIED R. VANHONACKER is an accomplished scholar, academic entrepreneur, and pedagogical innovator. He led and played a key role in the establishment of leading business schools in China (CEIBS, Shanghai) and in Russia (MSM SKOLKOVO, Moscow). He was the founding director of INSEAD's PhD program (Fontainebleau, France) and built the marketing department of the HKUST Business School (Hong Kong) into a noted academic research department. He holds a PhD in management (marketing science) from Purdue University (West Lafayette, Indiana, USA) and a licentiate in TEW (economometrics) from UFSIA (Antwerp, Belgium). He divides his time between Shanghai and the French countryside.